WHAT PEOPLE A

# THE TRANSFORMATIONAL TRUTH OF YOU!

"The universe has a wicked sense of humour"... It certainly does, and is portrayed wonderfully in this beautifully written book. Irony, humour, facts and an intelligent look at how we can change our lives for the better and how to work confidently with the challenges the Universe throws at us. Once started I could not put this book down. Highly recommended.
**Kim Arnold**, Founder of the UK Tarot Conference and Hay House Author

*The Transformational Truth of YOU!* shows us that the force of intention is the magic which manifests everything. Tiffany has the ability to take you on a soul journey like no other. This book empowered me to gain a deeper understanding of my own path and how to stay connected to it. Through profound metaphoric tales Tiffany sheds light on aspects of her own personal experience, with great exercises and powerful messages I felt Tiffany related to me. Her book is as personal and profound to her as it will be to you, the reader.
**Aldo Raffa**, Celebrity TV Psychic, www.aldoraffa.co.uk

For anyone who's drawn to the ideas behind The Law of Attraction this book will be a compelling read. Through her own stories and the archetypes of the Tarot's Major Arcana Tiffany Crosara raises important questions in her exploration of modern day "magick", returning us to our spiritual roots and revealing the alchemical powers within all of us.
**Joanna Watters**, Author of *Tarot for Today* & *Astrology for Today*, www.joannawatters.com

# The Transformational Truth of YOU!

## The Magician's Journey

# The Transformational Truth of YOU!

## The Magician's Journey

Tiffany Crosara

Winchester, UK
Washington, USA

First published by Axis Mundi Books, 2015
Axis Mundi Books is an imprint of John Hunt Publishing Ltd., Laurel House, Station Approach,
Alresford, Hants, SO24 9JH, UK
office1@jhpbooks.net
www.johnhuntpublishing.com
www.axismundi-books.com

For distributor details and how to order please visit the 'Ordering' section on our website.

Text copyright: Tiffany Crosara 2014

ISBN: 978 1 78279 755 5
Library of Congress Control Number: 2014956328

All rights reserved. Except for brief quotations in critical articles or reviews, no part of this book may be reproduced in any manner without prior written permission from the publishers.

The rights of Tiffany Crosara as author have been asserted in accordance with the Copyright, Designs and Patents Act 1988.

A CIP catalogue record for this book is available from the British Library.

Design: Lee Nash

Printed and bound in the USA by Edwards Brothers Malloy

We operate a distinctive and ethical publishing philosophy in all areas of our business, from our global network of authors to production and worldwide distribution.

# CONTENTS

*To love, life and the beautiful Co Creation of the 'Youniverse'.*

*To all of you who have been a part of my journey on this path, spirit, clients, colleagues, publishers, editors, family and friends, for being both visible and invisible guides of beauty on my path. And a special dedication to my daughter in spirit, Lauren Etienne Ronald, here's your message sweetheart, I'm paying it forward...*

# Foreword

For years I've taken for granted a somewhat synchronous life. I'm fortunate in that I rarely need to wait for something to manifest if I want it badly enough. This is both a blessing and detriment. The adage – 'be careful what you wish for', applies here. Admittedly, I'm guilty of not taking the time to understand why the Universe and I seem to work in tandem. The answer – 'we just do', no longer fits and really doesn't honour what's been given.

Since reading Tiffany Crosara's enlightening book, The Transformational Truth of You, I feel I can now give definition to my life experience and as a result, my limited focus has since widened, making room for integrity and inclusivity of the sacred to share the journey.

Tiffany provides a type of roadmap that keeps me on track with my personal mission and I can't help but see her as a skilled spiritual tour guide who lays the ground with doable checklists before, during and after the adventure. Each item helps build a more profound relationship with something greater and the ripple effect is palpable and transforming.

Along the journey Tiffany introduces useful tarot archetypes that motivate magic, love and abundance. Each encounter creates new pathways for navigating magical thinking and as an end result (or is it just the beginning?), a profound connection with your 'Youniverse' takes place. This is key to the journey as it delivered me to a place where I could soul-tend and make a difference.

If you are searching for a way to align with a supportive force that is universal and promotes unity, I encourage you to take up this adventure that Tiffany Crosara has thoughtfully laid out. A life changing adventure awaits and with it comes transforming results.

*Carrie Paris, Creator of The Magpie Oracle and The Lenormand Revolution Deck.*

www.carrieparis.com

# A Recipe for a Youniversal life...

Imagine your life is like baking a loaf of bread, you need the right ingredients to make it rise. To do this you start by...

**Chapter 1 (Justice) –** *Working Out the Karma in Your Story*
Weighing up all you have and getting real about what you can do with what you have and where you are...
Do have the right ingredients and in what proportion?
If you don't – can you get the information or ingredients?
Do you have the right equipment and environment?

**Chapter 2 (The Magician***) – Working Out the Consciousness in Unconsciousness*
When you have all of the above, you can bless what you have and honour the Co Creative alchemical process you are about to go through. Remember you didn't grow the wheat or evaporate the salt or make the yeast or draw the water, but through your skilful work and the ordinary ingredients you have gathered – and the amazing powers of yeast (ether), you will Co Create something delicious and life sustaining.

**Chapter 3 (Temperance***) – Sourcing Messages from the Past for the Future*
Start slowly take a deep breath in and feel the coolness of the flour in the bowl. Mix in the salt. Smell the flour; allow yourself to express whatever experience sparks to life inside you. Rise up to the call of "yeast-today". You take something that looks like dust (past), or a lump of clay if it's live yeast, and when you mix it with warm water (the flow) and sugar (sweetness) it suddenly comes alive and starts to make carbon dioxide (ether), frothing up the water with its liveliness (future).

**Chapter 4 (The Chariot)** – *Mixing and Mastering the Elements*
Breathe in, breathe out, apply your intention through your "knead" – aligned only to the highest good of all. Mix the yeast liquid with the flour and salt, knead the bread with your hands (about 10 minutes), rhythmically stretching and squashing it, making sure the yeast is completely mixed into the dough so it can do its work. Feel the chaos in Co Creation, the pressure, the mixing up, the mess, allow yourself to get deep into it, enjoy REALLY getting your hands dirty.

**Chapter 5 (The High Priestess)** – *Working with Imagination, Intention, Intuition, Integrity and the Id*
Now trust that all you need to know to make it rise is in the unseen process and journey of awareness – that is what yeast is and does. Your daily bread is all well within your care.

**Chapter 6 (Death) –** *Developing Truth, Trust and Transformation*
Clear the sticky mess of the past from your hands – gently. Put it in a bowl and cover it, look at it, and insert it into a special appliance ready for transformation to happen.

**Chapter 7 (The Wheel of Fortune)** – *Fulfilling Graceful Opportunities*
Leave it there and do something else. Release everything, just let it go – knowing that it's all part of the journey. Trust that the living yeast will make its air bubbles and the bread will rise by itself.

**Chapter 8 (The Sun)** – *Working with the Ether for What Matters' Sake*
When it has doubled in size, transfer your first process to a loaf-tin and place it in the hot oven. Set your intention of alchemy through the measure of heat and time (preheated oven at gas mark 6 for 40-45 minutes). Go and do something else, trusting the process will work as it has for thousands of years. The Sun

always rises (No peeking now – unless you want a flop or damaged eyes?).

**Chapter 9 (The Empress)** – *Developing a Youniversal Recipe for a Successful Career*
Come back at the allotted time to the wonderful smell of baking bread. Remove your first process from the oven, seeing the transformation and allowing it time to stand, cool off and set (make sure it sounds hollow when you tap the underside of it). Go slowly, take a deep breath and ... enjoy the first sight of your creation. Savour the moment. Even if the loaf isn't perfect – it's still your wonderful Co Creation. Share your Youniverse with the ones you love, feel the deep inner nurturing in shared connection.

**Chapter 10 (The Lovers)** – *Developing a Youniversal Recipe for Successful Relationships*
Draw in the irresistible scent of freshly baked bread wafting under your nostrils, feel the desire rising up within your body, your glands salivating at the need to taste, and quench the deep hollow emptiness within; sense the emotions taking possession of you, reverting your limbic mind to a mere animal instinctual state, or not as the case maybe ... depending on how much grace you have managed to muster throughout the creation of this transformational process. Perhaps you can even still go on sharing with others first, knowing and trusting that if you are meant to savour your creation, it will still be there, continually nourishing your life.

**Chapter 11 (The Star)** – *Finally, a Channelled Recipe for Igniting Your Youniverse*
Next time put away the recipe book and get playfully Co Creative. Experiment – try adding cheese or herbs or dried fruit or anything you fancy, knowing you have all this within.

# Introduction

## What is 'Youniversal' Co Creation?

The Transformational Truth of You is all about The Magician's Journey. The Magician has the power to manifest whatever he thinks – so it's really important he thinks the right thoughts.

My first book The Transformational Truth of Tarot (The Fool's Journey) was a rather effortless birth, just like The Fool itself, a bright breezy beginning born of only one draft.

So when I was prompted by my guides to write *The Transformational Truth of You* I expected it to be a similar process: One where I put pen to paper and just let it all hang out. After my first draft I put it out there into the world, feeling excited and expecting everyone to get it. But what I got back was showing me that the journey of the book wasn't clear, nobody felt they knew what Co Creation was from reading the book. After draft two and three I put it out there again and the feedback was "better, but still unclear". I felt as if I was being met with a huge challenge of how to get really clear with my communication – then it clicked! If ever I were ever to have that lesson, it would be in The Magician's journey! To be a true Magician we have to be a master of communication, and that is no easy feat – particularly when it comes to the intangible forces in the Universe. I felt I was being asked to describe something indescribable. Something I knew and felt right down to the core of my being and the marrow of my bones that I just didn't have words for. Just like the Hebrew name for God 'YHWH' is unpronounceable – if one tries to pronounce it then one simply ends up breathing! I was being asked, "What is Co Creation?" by some really big publishers – and all I could do was breathe!

Something just wasn't tangible enough. Re-write after re-write I was trying to convince myself that I had finally finished the manuscript, yet there was still some intangible suspended penny hanging around in my head that just wouldn't drop, no matter how much headbanging I did. I gave up trying to make it drop, and just as I was about to drop the manuscript into my publishers lap with the title 'The Transformational Truth of Co Creation' a series of events made the penny drop. I was at the time launching a new programme and asked for some feedback on the titles for it, the top two of which were The Transformational Truth of You, and The Transformational Truth of the Universe. I then cracked a joke about how maybe I should call it 'The Transformational Truth of the Youniverse' and suddenly the whole group latched onto the term 'Youinverse' saying it struck a deep cord of recognition within. So even the story about the final title of this book is an example of how Co Creation works. Co Creation is the connection between you and the Universe that ignites the 'Youniversal' creation.

Allow yourself to listen with your heart and your feelings throughout the book, travel down the pages of The Transformational Truth of You, and your life, and see what opens up for you.

My intention with The Transformational Truth of You is to attempt to pin down the elusory nature of the infinite experience and perception by means of a guided journey of self-discovery. I propose to immerse you, the reader, into a pool of mythological experience as a lucid medium to facilitate discovering parts of yourself that may once have lain dormant. I seek to take you on a shared experience that I undertook myself, to help you see and connect with yourself. Bringing realization of just how much you may have been missing, and just how much more you can realize within yourself once you know more of who you are. And that is the key, self-acceptance of who you are, right now. The ability to see it, to own it, not try to change it in a forced, heavy stressful manner, but with clarity of knowing where your journey is evolving to.

Life is for living – life is for Co Creating, life is for recognizing and rejoicing in the connection between yourself and the Universe, to such an extent that you merge your own inner potential with the boundless possibilities of the Universe and become truly 'Youniversal'.

### Co Creation is The Magician's Journey...

Co Creation is the journey of realization; realization that you are more than just 'you', therefore your life is more than your own. You are not in control of your life like you might think you are. Co Creation is the journey of realization that there is something bigger at work here. You are in a partnership with the Universe, you are a part of it to such a degree that you and the Universe are one, just like the number of The Magician in the Tarot. One represents the journey of the self – The Transformational Truth of You! You are in a relationship with the Universe, but because the Universe is literally everything, we tend to see it all around us, rather than our direct connectedness to it. We often walk around thinking our own thoughts are our own thoughts and our own feelings are our own feelings, that our creations are our own creations and therefore so are our manifestations, and they are – partially, but first and foremost they came from the Universe.

See yourself as a receiver satellite dish on the Earth and the Universe as a satellite in space. Through experience with my guides that is how I perceive that Co Creation works; you receive the information from the Universal satellite. However a satellite doesn't have an ego, but we humans do, so we identify with the information, and we make it our own. We forget that it's being broadcast out to humanity, and that certain satellites (humans, animals, plants, even minerals) pick up on the certain frequencies (whatever they are tuned in to). Some satellites are turned off completely. But once we wake up to the realization that this communication is coming from the Universe we can then open our energies up to more and more magical frequencies and possibilities. The space satellite Universe needs the Earth satellites to do something with the information; this is how it creates, through Co Creation with its Earth satellites (humans and all other organisms). Of Earth's satellite receptors, humans hold the most responsibility for the wellbeing of the Earth's resonance, so it is important for our receptors to become open, clear and functioning healthily. The Transformational Truth of You is designed to facilitate the opening and clear functioning of our human facility as satellite receptors, in order to absorb and interpret the vast array of cosmic consciousness being conveyed by the Universe's beacons.

### "So is Co Creation 'The Law of Attraction'?"

Co Creation is similar to The Law of Attraction, but (in a very basic generalisation) The Law of Attraction can be described as thinking about what you want and setting out to attract it. Co Creation is about realizing that your thoughts and desires are not actually your own, first and foremost. The emphasis is on your connection with Creation, which is a very important and overlooked fundamental part of attracting good karma and not having the repercussions that can come about when you are just creating from your own will/desires/ego. This may sound contradictory because I said our desires are not our own, so let me explain.

In the pure first arrival of thought and desire, thought and desire are not our own – inspiration comes from spirit (in-spirit-ation) but the ego identifies, attaches, and we get into problems, because essentially speaking we have lost our alignment. The Transformational Truth of You focuses on keeping your alignment, when we do that we feel good, in fact we feel great! We feel magical and connected to all things seen and unseen, the excitement of endless possibilities lay before us and we feel we are doing the right thing and everything is flowing. Whereas with The Law of Attraction if we haven't learnt and understood that our thoughts and desires are channelled through to us, the attachment and identification can make us feel as if we are trying to push something uphill. We forget the source of the creation, and concentrate only on making the creation happen, causing attachment, anxiety, obsession, tiredness, exhaustion and an increasing feeling of separation and struggle. This is the exact opposite of what The Law of Attraction is creating, but the human condition finds it very hard to focus on something and then let it go if there isn't enough focus or understanding on the how or why we should let go.

### What is The Magician's Journey?

The ability to realize that by working with your karma and not against it you become a channel for the Universe's will, rather than your own. By doing so you unlock your true purpose for your existence, you get to know you and the Universe, and through honouring that and working with it, your life becomes magical, igniting the 'Youniverse'.

In that answer I realized I needed to work through my karma in order for this book to be born. It wasn't such a straightforward breeze! The ability to recognize your karma takes a lot of deep soul searching, facing hard truths and the ability and determination to keep revisiting and learning from it.

The process isn't easy and it isn't quick. Yet in today's society we are told that it is. That being our own Magician, we can have anything we want, and we have the ability to conjure it up out of the air. And whilst this is not untrue, it can make pretty hollow unaligned creation if we aren't working with it from a deeprooted source of our own soul's history. Karma is our roots; we must remember and honour where we have come from and our journey of growth if we are going to grow to our fullest potential and purpose. I use trees quite a bit as an analogy in this book and the first point about them I will bring your attention to is that the deeper and stronger a tree's roots are, the more it can rise up and open out to the heavens. It is important to emphasise here that I am talking about the soul's roots and soul purpose, which goes back further than wherever your origin may be in this life. I imagine that the individual tree does not know its family tree! It doesn't know all of its ancestry but it does know its roots and connection to the Earth. You existed before this life, that is how far your roots go back and that is the depth of knowing I am talking about. Our identity and purpose is something that has been developing for lifetimes. Knowing our identity/purpose and how it works with the world in order to grow to our absolute best is essential; otherwise, somewhere along the trunk, we just become a branch, a disembodied arm just grabbing at something, anything – a top-heavy tree about to topple over. By not looking at and admitting we have karma, we add to it in an unhealthy manner – we don't transform it at all. When that happens our manifestations get loaded with negative karma and then we wonder why it didn't happen in the way we wanted it to!

Life is a collection of experiences through which we can identify the process of our karma. When gathering our stories together from all over the place we end up with a jumble of incoherent snapshots of who we are; the picture just isn't clear. It takes a lot of reflective visits to make sense of it. I am hoping that my revisits to The Transformational Truth of You have now helped me form a clear picture of my own identity, soul's roots and path, and I hope through sharing it that it will equally support your journey to discover your identity and soul's roots and path.

The journey involves navigating through eleven chapters. The number eleven is the first of the master numbers and a very magical number. But besides this, to me eleven is the number of the Youniverse (1 for you, and 1 for the Universe = 11 = Youinverse). If you know yourself you become a defined entity, a channel, you become like an aerial. When an aerial is straight up like a number 1, it receives information clearly, seemingly from nowhere. But it isn't from nowhere, it's from a broadcaster, another defined source, and this source I will refer to as the Universe for the purpose of the book. Put them together (you and the Universe) and you get Co Creation, which in turn leads to being the Youniverse. When you have Co Creation, you and your life are in alignment, and when that happens any desire that is evolutionary and for the highest good of all becomes totally possible.

The chapters are all identified by a different step in the process of making bread. Making bread is a metaphor I am using to demonstrate the different stages in Co Creation (rising up to a transformative life).

Each chapter/recipe instruction is assigned a Tarot card for those of you that are that way inclined. Even though the Tarot is mentioned in parts of the book, it is merely employed as an archetypal teaching tool that will speak to you through your subconscious. You do not need to understand Tarot to understand The Transformational Truth of You.

Each chapter has a story. It may be a true-life story, or a metaphorical story. Both serve the intention of speaking to you through your eyes and your heart. Creating a vision, a feeling, a knowing. Demonstrating where the knowledge is coming from, what the journey of Co Creation is about, and an understanding of how and why it works. There is no need to go into the story so that you can understand how it relates to Co Creation immediately, as it will be revealed to you in the exercises afterwards. Just relax and enjoy the story.

The exercises are meant to feed your thoughts so that you can reflect on what stories of Co Creation you have had and to help you to identity your karma and work with it consciously. Once karma is faced without resistance a process of unblocking happens, unlocking your true calling, purpose and identity. Without knowing your karma you have nothing to work with – with knowledge of your karma you have everything to work for.

May your life be one filled with magical transformation, truth and Co Creation.

## Chapter 1

# Justice

### Working Out the Karma in Your Story

> *Make no mistakes about it – enlightenment is a destructive process. It has nothing to do with becoming better or happier. Enlightenment is the crumbling away of untruth. Seeing through the façade of pretence. It's the complete eradication of everything we believed to be true.*
> – Adyashanti

Do you sometimes think that another way to spell life could be I.R.O.N.I.C?

Perhaps you have just decided to become vegan and the Universe puts you in an environment of meat eaters, or you start a job as a traffic warden and you end up with more of your own unpaid parking tickets than ever before.

You give up chocolate, and for your birthday the only presents you get are Milk Tray.

You win some money when automatically entered into a prize draw at an airport, but you miss the train to the airport on the return journey and get a taxi, which rips you off for that exact amount just to find that your plane was delayed anyway!

Perhaps you make a vow never to go on holiday to a particular destination again, but a series of circumstances means you end up going there more than any other destination.

Maybe you move somewhere to be closer to your work office and as soon as you put a deposit down you get an email notifying you that your work office is moving.

Or you say to your friends you would never move somewhere in particular and then they all end up moving there, so you do and then they all move away!

All of the above are actual examples from my own life, apart the traffic warden and parking tickets – and hopefully it stays that way!

The Universe introduced me to the man who is my husband three years before I met him properly. He walked into the shop I owned, had a cuppa in the chill-out basement and then left. I remember thinking, "I hope he comes back in to the shop." He never did. But as soon as I shut shop I went in another shop and he walked in!

My husband spent his younger life inspired by Rastafarian philosophy, which led him to be a vegetarian for sixteen years. He grew up in multi-cultural South London and was dead against freemasonry, which he saw as the Illuminati, and he was totally Ital (eating food celebrated by the Rastafari movement – no fizzy drinks, no processed foods, just strictly healthy). So how ironic that he married a country butcher's granddaughter whose family has members who are part of a lodge, then he became a meat eater and I became vegan! The first time he met my family was at a lodge charity event. Meat was put in front of him after saying grace (ironic?) I told him to push it on to my plate – he didn't. He told me it was in front of him so he was going to eat it and that was that; sixteen years of vegetarianism came to an end that day. He wondered if he should be vegetarian after that but he just kept getting messages that it was time to eat meat, even from Jehovah Witnesses that would turn up at his door and quote messages from the bible about how eating meat was fine! However if you would have said to him that he was going to marry a butcher's granddaughter who struggled with vegetables and was addicted to processed foods, sugar, fizzy drinks and barely knew what reggae was, he would have laughed and said, "No way!" Now I am more Ital and he is more give and take. Is this what the irony of life is about? Does it stop us from becoming too rigid, from shrivelling up and drying out?

The irony in life is a funny thing indeed. Why is it here? Is it karma or coincidence? Is it a sardonic reminder that we don't know what is best?

Are we so "hell-bent" as humans on things being a particular way that we need the spirit of irony to set us straight, humbling our own arrogant and ignorant ways? We weren't born knowing that the Universe knows best – well most us weren't. We have to learn it, and we learn it through the spirit of irony it seems. Learning through Irony is the training for becoming a conscious Co Creator, teaching us the price of becoming too attached.

You could see irony as an angel, a guide, or one of God's messengers. God saying to him, "See Mr Jo Bloggs down there, Irony, he is getting too stuck in his ways, his head is getting full of judgments and opinions, go and pay him a visit!" Then God sits back in his big golden throne, stroking his long silvery beard and munching on popcorn whilst he enjoys the show. "God laughs at those who make plans" so they say, but I for one don't believe for a minute that this is for "entertainment purposes only". In the psychic work I do we have to use that very line "for entertainment purposes only" yet we all know it's anything but! Really it's a god damn (excuse the French/pun) serious business passing on messages to increase collective consciousness, but somehow entertainment comes along for the ride! This is how I see the spirit of irony and I wonder if you will too as you read through the sometimes archetypal and sometimes true stories contained in these pages. It may seem like it's for entertainment purposes only, but it's really a lot more than that!

One of my intentions with this book is to get you thinking about how irony has paid you a visit in your life and what the outcome has been. For instance, a Reiki student of mine gave someone healing and he was feeling bad because the client's hip had popped during the session. His client had then popped along to the hospital with his popped hip and someone at the hospital said, "It's good you popped out and popped in now because if this had gone undetected for any longer there would have been serious implications." In Reiki we are told just to give/send healing without attaching ourselves to what we think should be the outcome. To stay open, to be a channel for the highest good, to state that we cannot possibly know what that is and live by that practice. It can be hard to have that level of trust – my student was scared he had done something to his client's hip, but we have to take a deep breath and let go of what we think, and any judgments around it. The philosophy of Reiki is a perfect example of what I am trying to say here.

I remember when my granddad had a heart attack at the same time a couple of hospitals had closed in the area, resulting in a huge backlog for treatment. Whenever I went to see him he looked fine so I didn't send him any healing, knowing that it works for the highest good and if the highest good was for him to pop off the planet I couldn't deal with that. So I decided not to fix what wasn't broken. But he ended up trapped in hospital like it was a never-ending prison sentence with only one repetitive sentence…

"Your operation won't be today, Mr Read, maybe tomorrow"…

This was all he had heard for six weeks and he was becoming increasingly upset and depressed, he just wanted to go home. So I decided it was time and sent him some distance healing before I went to bed one night. When I fell asleep I had a dream that he visited me and asked me what I had just done, so I said, "It's okay, Granddad, just a bit of healing, go back to bed." Three days later I got a call from my mum saying that the hospital decided that he didn't need the operation after all and could go home. But we still felt that something wasn't right. A few days after he arrived home the hospital decided he did need the operation after all, and because they had messed him around so much they were going to pay for him to go private, meaning he could stay at home until he was called in. Now we would have never in a million years seen that coming, and the amount of facing the fear to deal with what could have happened was immense for me; it took a lot to say okay, I let go, and trust that whatever happens will come to pass.

I see this challenge in a multitude of different ways in all of our lives today. We get stuck on our lives having to be in a certain routine or our partners having to behave a certain way to feel safe. But nothing could be further than the truth. It's very much an illusion. I wish to share with you ways to Co Create peace, beauty and harmony in our lives. It always comes down to one thing – grace. In a way grace and irony go hand in hand, irony teaches us to be graceful. Giving us the chance to navigate around something we didn't see coming, practicing the art of respecting that if it is there, it has every right to be there. It is a fundamental lesson in trusting that the Universe is always working for our highest good, even if it doesn't feel like it. In fact it's often when it doesn't feel like life's difficult circumstances are working for the highest good that our karma is being afforded the most healing.

My intent with this book is that through sharing some of my own real life or archetypal stories you will be able to identify with your own ironic, karmic, angel of grace and hear the message it is delivering to you. My wish is that after reading this book you are in such an aligned place that you can let go of all that feels heavy, stressful or out of balance in your life, knowing that the reason you hang on to it (the need for security) is an illusion.

I can't stress how important it is to face our truth, our karma, our past, our attachments, no matter how scary. If we just pretend it isn't there and keep on going for what we want, then a karmic car crash is just waiting to happen from not looking in our mirrors and turning the wheel in the direction we think is best when we still have blinkers on. Whether it's that heart attack from the stress of being at the office all the time when you would really prefer to be at home writing your novel. Or the upset of finding your partner in bed with your best friend when you knew there was something up there all along but never wanted to face it. We stay in these heavy situations because we want to attain some type of security, even though they make us desperately unhappy. Ultimately we don't get the security anyway, because if we are desperately unhappy then the angel of irony will come and give us a wake-up call. So let's turn around, look our karma deeply in the eye and wink at the angel of irony in all its glory.

Below I am going to share a story from my life, one of the biggest stories of my life, if not the biggest. The one that made me the bulk of who I am today, the one that turned my life right around, this story is the backbone threading its way through this book. It's been my greatest teacher and, as you read it, I hope that it gets you thinking about what your biggest story and teacher in your life has been. There will be exercises to help you with that afterwards so please do not strain, just have a relaxed intent as you read.

## Getting to Know Your Relationship with Your Youniverse

**The Devil** – *Fear*

Fifteen-year-old Snow White, had seven inner-child dwarves, called Despair, Loneliness, Depression, Anxiety, Rage, Obsession and Compulsion, which resulted in an eighth called Disorder. Snow White struggled with these dwarves so much that everybody saw she was unworthy of such a name. But thankfully most of her time was spent alone, which was some kind of damage limitation – for others, but not so for Snow.

One day Snow got up and, as usual, Loneliness, Obsession, Compulsion, Anxiety and Disorder had such a strong morning presence. She went to the bathroom to brush her teeth and heard, "Brush your teeth thoroughly and gently because if your gums bleed that means your mum is going to die in a car crash." Snow looked at her train tracks in the mirror and began the complicated task – at last she finished. "Well, you passed that one," she heard. "But now you have to run down the stairs in less than twenty seconds, without tripping just to make sure." Again Snow passed this, she was getting good at all these tests. She had to. More and more new ones were appearing every day, and she hated the way the voice lied to her all the time. The tests never really ended, she never really passed. She was a slave to the liar within, and although she knew it was a liar, Anxiety wouldn't let Obsession, Compulsion or Disorder go. Anxiety loved to feed them, make them bigger and fatter, so Anxiety could make itself indispensable.

"Now for the boiled egg test," she hears.

"So if it cracks, what's going to be the punishment today? Is it that my only parent will die? Or the bullies at school will beat me up again? Or that my new found boyfriend will go off with my best friend – again?"

"Right first time," says the voice

"But I've already passed two tests to save my mum's life?"

"Ever heard of third time lucky?"

Snow watches the egg boiling, the mantra of "Please don't crack, please don't crack, please don't crack," an endless chant escaping her lips ... the pressure rising and ... smack! It cracks. Snow hears the disembodied laugh echoing around her head, and as if she was the egg, she cracks...

**The High Priestess** – *Inner Voice*

Coming round in slow motion, Snow is witnessing all the destruction she is causing in the kitchen through utter rage and frustration, as if she is in the third person. The reason she comes round is because she is slowly noticing that everything she's throwing gets thrown back at her. Either by bouncing back, or by knocking something else that causes a domino effect.

At first the physical knocks and increasing injustice makes her feel justifiably enraged, but the madder she gets, the worse it comes back at her.

In utter desperation she cries out, "Why, why?" and to her surprise she hears a different voice. One that is strong, deep, calm and wise. Not an uptight trickster. One she knows she can trust.

"Snow, all the time you focus on what is wrong, the worse it gets."

Snow stopped.

**The Hanged Man** – *Escapism*

The next morning Snow got up, to the trickster voice of Obsession, Compulsion and Disorder, who were waiting with more tests than ever before. But now Snow began to see through these tests. Snow still needed to do them, but where there was uncontrollable Fear and Rage if she lost, she now kept calm. She was booting Anxiety and Rage out, and as she did there was no feeder for Obsession, Compulsion and Disorder. As they shrank, the trickster voice petered out into a whisper that Snow was not going to strain herself to hear.

Even so, this was just the start of a long journey of consciousness for Snow. One plagued with deep pitfalls along the way. The dwarves of Despair and Depression still hung out in her space, and would trip her up with experiences of both legal and illegal drugs, sleeping around, binge-drinking, comfort eating and general low self-esteem. After one particular episode Snow White was given the kiss of life, not by her prince, but by a big thick plastic tube being forced past the gag reflex of her throat. She realized she was the one feeding Depression and Despair. She stopped binge-drinking, eating and (legal) drug taking.

Depression and Despair still had residence, but the fact that she no longer fed them meant they decreased in size, and she began to feel better. It was the two steps forward, one step back tango we all know so well, but she was getting better with practice at not concentrating on what was wrong, just letting wrong be wrong... But still, nothing felt right.

She had acquired two new dwarves; both with a double-barrelled name of 'Illegal-Drugs' and another called 'Sleeping-Around', but these were at least fun – for a while.

**Strength** – *Responsibility*

At nineteen Snow found out she was pregnant. Dossing with friends, and in a newly formed relationship with the nineteen-year-old father who could be whisked off by the army at any moment, it wasn't a fairy tale scene.

Snow, who had won a pro-abortion debate at school, found herself in a position where she could not dream of terminating her child's young life for the sake of her own not so old life. Snow found an uncanny amount of strength within to stand up and say, "Do whatever you need to, whatever happens I am stopping the drugs and keeping this baby." And that she did. Until her daughter's life was "cut short" four months after her birth. In a panic the healthcare services put the grieving childless mother Snow White on hard-core legal drugs. And yes, for the first two years Snow really did want to die each day, and the dwarf of Death hung over her like a cloud of musty suffocating cold and damp. No escape from him even in her sleep; each night she dreamt of the death over and over again and when she woke the dwarf of death was looming over her as soon as she opened her eyes. His eyes drilling into hers with the mantra, "Remember, relive, like it just happened." Snow wanted to die, but she knew she wouldn't. She had found a new strength, a strength that hadn't left with her daughter's body, a strength that her daughter seeded deep into her womb and left behind. Snow noted the strength from the beginning of the pregnancy, which in itself was an experience loaded with illness, strange occurrences and drama. The journey through the birth and life of her child demanded all the Strength that Snow could muster, and muster strength Snow did. Through her newfound strength, Snow found life, and brought forth life.

**The Fool** – *The Unexpected*

The first synchronistic and strange encounter happened when Snow was six weeks pregnant. A stranger came up to her and asked her how the baby was. Stunned, Snow replied, "I don't have a baby."

The Irish Leprechaun like archetype stood in front of her, looked her deep in the eyes (Snow White is only short herself) and said, "Oh, come on now, just because you're only six weeks pregnant, it doesn't mean you don't have one!"

"Do I know you?" replied Snow

"Do you know me?" asked Leprechaun

"No!"

"But I know you are pregnant, and I know the baby will be born on November 24th – tell me I am right, tell me I am right!"

(Leprechaun starts jumping up and down)

"No! You aren't! It's November 9th actually."

"Ah, that's what the doctors say!" he said, walking away.

Well, Snow's daughter was overdue, and had to be booked in for induction. Standing at the hospital counter with her mother, their eyes scanning the pages that were flipping rapidly in the receptionist's diary, a big round weary Snow turns to her mum and whispers, "I knew it, she isn't coming until the 24th." Her mum doesn't respond, her eyes glued on the turning pages. As Snow looks, a page lands open with the date 24th November. "I am afraid we don't have anything until 24th November," says the receptionist.

**The Chariot** – *The Uncontrollable*

On the 24th November, Snow had her waters broken which resulted quickly in being rushed in for emergency caesarean, due to the baby being in distress. She already knew this was possible. The pregnancy had been plagued by bizarre health happenings, but nothing was ever voiced by anyone on the outside, it was her own inner voice that informed her.

A team of white coats swirled around her like a tornado, ripping off her jewellery, another administering a mixture of injections, gas and air. Forms and pens dancing frantically in front of her face, voices saying, "Quickly sign here," the baby's father being held at bay as the tornado hurricanes through the hospital hall. In the operating theatre Snow looks at the nurse, tears burning her eyes ... and then ... she feels ... that she stopped existing...

**The Moon** – *Confusion and Sedation*

Coming round she hears her first husband's voice. "Snow, Snow, look we've got a beautiful baby girl..." Snow comes round to a Polaroid picture. Quickly he explains, "She is in intensive care, because she flat-lined at birth and they had to resuscitate her, but she's all right. I've called her Lauren Etienne after St Etienne! Ya ma's with her now!" he says, waving the polaroid excitedly, accompanied only by a big fat beaming Cheshire (well Glaswegian) grin.

So Lauren was named Lauren Etienne meaning 'Victorious Crown'. Not that we knew that at the time, the only conscious reason was because her dad liked the name Lauren and St Etienne was his favourite group! His favourite album was 'Too Young To Die'. It wasn't until after Lauren Ettiene did just that, that Snow read the back of the album:

> *"Like coming from a Cinema matinee in broad daylight, St Etienne stands before you blinking and disorientated, but happy. And already you miss them, before they've even gone. And yet you want them to leave, so you can get on with the serious business of missing them, too late to say goodbye, but too young to die."*

"Woah ... this is trippy," a morphine induced Snow thinks to herself, as the Polaroid starts to get eaten up by orange Scorpions that had a liking for doner kebabs! The Scorpions must have been hungry, because they stayed with Snow all day, as did the never-ending self-regenerating doner kebabs! The day entered the time zone of eons, each minute equalling an hour. Snow would close her eyes and think she was out of it for two hours, then she would wake due to a visit from mum or her husband and they would inform her they had only been gone ten minutes (not quite a minute an hour, but I'm dramatic).

**The Empress** – *Love and Protection*

It wasn't until the day after that Snow was conscious enough to be moved from her bed into a wheelchair to meet her daughter. Wheeled into SCBU, she was parked up in front of a glass case typical to the Snow White family line. Inside, her daughter's tiny Snow White body was being preserved, a little hole present in the glass where Snow could reach in and touch her – once her hands had been sanitised. Her daughter's chest rose and fell with all her might, her tiny sleeping body, linked up to tubes and wires. When Snow had first laid eyes on the Polaroid she had felt a love like never before, but now a bond had taken hold of her that couldn't ever tear her away, even though she was well aware of the fragility of life lying in front of her.

A voice jolts her back to the present. "Snow, are you sure you didn't get your dates wrong? She's awfully premature," says a nurse.

"No, I didn't get my dates wrong," she answers defiantly. Snow wasn't so great at being defiant and confident, and as the words escaped her mouth she was shocked at the force.

**The Tower** – *Shock*

Five days later Snow finds her daughter out of the incubator, filled with elation, she takes this as a great sign. Desperate to pick up her daughter and hold her for the first time, she is pulled into the consulting room before she gets a chance.

"Snow, your daughter has Edwards' Syndrome."

"Oh." Snow's heart sinks, but remembering not to focus on what is wrong, "At least it's not Down's."

"It's worse than Down's."

Snow can't believe her ears, but as she thinks that the consultant continues...

"The pair of chromosomes Lauren inherited from you and her father split incorrectly, causing a third chromosome. Dr Edwards found this chromosome, of which the number is 18. Dr Down found Chromosome 21. People know of Down's because children with Down's live through infancy. Children with Edwards' syndrome ... don't.

"However, in Lauren's case, two wrongs made a partial right. The cells split again and evened back out. This means she has Mosaic Edwards' Syndrome. It's incredibly rare for a child with Edwards' Syndrome to go full term. Let alone for cells to split incorrectly twice and create a mosaic.

"Not a lot of doctors even know of this syndrome, and we have only ever had one case here since the hospital began over 100 years ago. Not only that but Lauren isn't the only one in the hospital with Edwards' syndrome right now, we have also in SCBU, another baby girl, who has just been born with full Edwards' syndrome. I will put you in touch with her parents, but be warned. Do not look for information on Edwards' syndrome, as it will only pull you down.

"As Lauren is mosaic we will need to run a number of tests to find out what parts of her are and aren't affected. However, although she has a milder form of Edwards' syndrome, we still don't expect her to live past the age of three."

Snow rushes out of the consultants room, feeling so light-headed, she stops in her tracks as she feels she is about to faint – a mixed reaction from the amount of blood she lost in the caesarean and the shock of being dropped from a great height. One minute elated that her daughter is out of the incubator, the next finding out it's because sooner, and not later, she will die. Appearances can be so deceptive.

A nurse catches up with her. "Come and hold your daughter."

Defiance again, shocking them both, this time a loud blow from just two letters, "NO!"

Snow rushes back to her room, barely keeping consciousness. It's a cold, grey November afternoon, what little sun there is weakened by city hospital walls, fading fast, just like hope itself. The room feels more like a prison cell than a hospital room. The walls cave in on her with claustrophobic darkness, so heavy, and so suffocating, oppression bears down on her hard. And once again she hears the same voice that saved her once before. "This is it, Snow, one way or another, which way are you going to go?"

The pressure of the darkness grows in such force that it expels Snow through the door and she uses that force to run back to SCBU as fast as she can.

She picks up her daughter and holds her for the first time. A radio is on and Robbie Williams' 'Angels' begins playing simultaneously – it was one of the first ever airtime plays.

But Snow really knew she had turned a corner when a nurse said to her, "You must be thinking, why you?" She replied, "Actually, I was thinking why not me? I know it's me because I can love her more than anyone else could."

And love Lauren more than anyone else possibly could was something Snow dedicated the whole of herself to. For the first time in her life she was not self-obsessed, she was of true service. For the first time Snow no longer behaved like the world owed her something and she began living as if she owed the world something.

Snow made a conscious decision to open her heart completely, and love her daughter with all of it – even while knowing that she was going to lose her.

**The Star** – *Release*

From that day on Snow met the inner dwarves of Grace, Decorum and Humility. And from that day on her life did turn around, slowly but surely. Snow's life has continued on the path of strong initiations, but now she knows she has choice about how she lives through them. Snow, at the time of writing this, was thirty-six; by then she had lost a lot of loved ones, and had an incredible number of psychic experiences. At twenty-one, twenty-eight and thirty-five (every seven years) those experiences entwined for months on end and sent her to a deeply challenged place. A place where it felt as though her whole life was slipping away from her, but she once again came through. And each time she has come through more and more blessed.

Snow now spends her time divided between London and Cornwall. For her, London is a deeply magical ground of synchronicity, soul group encounters, creativity, evolution, transformation and opportunity. And for those reasons it occupies a big part of her heart that pumps the lifeblood through her veins.

Cornwall holds another big part of her heart, in the form of her prince, her stepdaughter, and her black cat familiar Mystic Mog – oh and Prince Tomcat too.

Snow knows that there is an extraordinary amount of magic in life, and that the more open we are to it, the more it happens. Sometimes magical happenings are incredibly challenging but if we keep going with it, doing our best to honour what is occurring, then the occurrences have the potential to turn into some massive blessing in the end.

I want to share with you how I work with karma, in order to transform it truly into 'real' blessings. Which doesn't just mean concentrating on what we want and manifesting that. It means being brave enough to take a long, hard, deep look at what life is presenting to us. To stand naked, to learn that what we have been given is exactly right for us, and to see why that is.

## What's the Karma in Your Story?

1. Pick a time in your life that you feel really defined who you are. The top one that stands out to you, your story. Get a pen and paper or a computer and get it out there, out of your head on to something you can see staring back at you.

2. Identify the different stages of the journey and what they showed you. You could place subtitles at each part (if you are Tarot orientated you could also title them a Tarot card that resonates with you. Or if you are oracle card orientated you might like to do the same). Write your subtitles down in whichever way that you can identify them for you right now. Perhaps it's even flowers, allow yourself to imagine and play, find a form of expression that speaks to you and allow yourself to be creative and think outside the box. Choose whatever vehicle best reflects your guided journey.

3. Looking at each stage, identify at least one word to describe what it felt like going through the experience. As a clear example of what I am asking, I have illustrated below by means of a chart my own story as embodied through my association with figures from the Tarot. As explained before you don't have to know the Tarot to do this. Just give each stage of your experience a name that resonates for you, and then contemplate what the learning came about from the experience and write it down.

| STAGE | LEARNING |
|---|---|
| Devil | Fear |
| The High Priestess | Inner voice |
| The Hanged Man | Escapism |
| Strength | Responsibility |
| The Fool | The unexpected |

| | |
|---|---|
| The Chariot | The uncontrollable |
| The Moon | Confusion and sedation |
| The Empress | Love and protection |
| The Tower | Shock |
| The Star | Release |

The purpose of mapping out your experience in this way is to bring shape and clarity to your karmic journey of life experiences. Can you see what your main story is about? For instance, by looking at the chart above I can see that my journey was about learning to let go of fear, control, obsession and attachment, and that my journey had moments of realisation, followed by a period of being tested, through to release.

From that you can begin to work out your karma. For instance, by looking through the above list I can identify here that my karma was/is about trying to control everything because of the immense fear within, the worst possible fear for a parent, had to happen for me to transform.

Your story contains your purpose or your gift. For example, my story identifies my need to control through feeling so out of control; so much controlling behaviour came in that it was severely unhealthy. Until a very strong situation happened to me that I could not control (my daughter being born terminally ill). The karma of control kept coming round harder and harder until it seemed it couldn't get any harder. Now I am not saying I am free of being controlling, but I am more conscious of it. I can see when it comes into play and I can consciously work to choose another way once I have seen it. I can and do practice letting go. By doing so I aid others in recognising their need to control, and help them to release themselves from that – thus my karma now becomes my purpose. I do this because feeling free of control and ultimately fear is an incredible feeling of bliss. Bliss is real, it exists, yet we may rarely access this state; by releasing fear and control we access the bliss state much quicker, easier and far more often.

## Experience Your Karmic Roots

Another way to find the karma in your story is to work with past life regression. Reincarnation was something I was not convinced about until I had a spontaneous past life recall at twenty-eight, which gave me names, dates and places that tied in exactly with the historical research I did afterwards. That experience led me to train as a past life regression therapist. Since then I have realized that all of the things I do or I am, are about the past and clearing the patterns of the past. That is what it all boils down to if we are to be unhindered on our journey of evolution. I have found past life regression to be one of the most powerful, if not the most powerful ways of doing this, because you experience it first hand for yourself. The only challenge is remaining open enough for the information to filter through from the sub-conscious. There are many ways of accessing past lives; from setting an intention to dreaming about them and to letting yourself daydream.

I would suggest you playfully explore some past life memories before doing the following exercise, as you will know then that you have not been influenced by what you may have found out astrologically. Instead I would expect the astrology to confirm what came up for you.

## The Reflection Karma in Your Youniverse

The ancient art of astrology is as infinite as the Universe itself, but with today's modern world it can be easier than ever to be your own basic astrologer really quickly. Your karmic story can be easily decoded in a few taps on your keyboard. Let me share with you how.

Go to www.astro.com

Go to create a horoscope and then to 'guest profile'.

Fill in the necessary details, if you don't know your time of birth then set it for midday or dowse or use your intuition, then click continue.

Go to horoscope chart drawings and then "chart drawing, ascendant" and click.

Now you should be able to see your chart. On the left there is a little box with the sign and name of each planet, and the zodiac sign the planet is found in within your chart.

The biggest karmic indicators are –

- The Moon – which stands for our deepest recesses of our psyche, the subconscious, our primal emotions, our mother and our past.
- Chiron – the wounded healer, wherever Chiron appears in your chart – that is where your karmic wound is. By finding and healing the wound in yourself your wound then becomes your gift in the world (you become the wounded healer).
- The Nodes – The true/north node is where your soul is heading, your evolutionary path. Directly opposite is the south node, where your soul has been, but for some reason it's never put on a chart! Basically your south node will always be opposite your north node.

Once you have spotted where they are, go on to a search engine and put in 'karmic astrology moon' – followed by whatever your sign is (indicated by the dots) and do the same for at least Chiron. You may be tempted to do the nodes as well.

If you want to take it further you can also add in the houses. The houses look like pieces of a pie in your chart, they have a number near the centre (basically, house one starts at what we would see as nine o clock and they work round anticlockwise). Look at the box in the top left to find the symbol (glyph) for the planet and then find which piece of the pie it is in, then pop it into a search engine "karmic astrology moon in Leo 8th house" for example.

Compare what appears in your astrology chart with what came up in your past life regression, it is likely to be very illuminating!

## Chapter 2

# The Magician

### Working Out the Consciousness in Unconsciousness

*Life has its rhythm and we have ours. They're designed to coexist in harmony, so that when we do what is ours to do and otherwise let life be, we gain acceptance and serenity.*
– Victoria Moran

I wonder if you feel that we can have an idea of what we want and even get a measure of success with it, but the process tends to feel heavy or blocked in some way, or we get it, but not in the way we wanted?

I tend to see that occurring a lot and I believe it is due to our reluctance to face ourselves and do the necessary inner work. To do so may require that we face the past, which may mean taking a path of destruction/clearing/changing/re-routing. One of the reasons why I think The Law of Attraction was so popular is because it felt as though we didn't need to look at the past. And that was so very refreshing after the therapy era of being told we need counselling to overcome our woes – and it will take years! The pendulum swung perhaps a little too far one way and then the other, now I hope we are coming into balance.

Our past journey holds the clues to our future journey. Without the grounding of knowing where we are building from, we are ungrounded, and are building bridges in an indistinct sky – bloody hard work, impossible even! We must honour where we are, look at what led us to where we are, take in the current landscape, look across at where we want to be and do the necessary work if we want to have a life full of progression and evolution. This is the recipe for all success; there is no big magical secret with that. Common sense is needed in all walks of life and especially when we are consciously working with the Universe for our soul's highest potential; doing so is a form of magic and when practicing magic it is paramount to remain grounded. It is my belief that The Law of Attraction is actually a modern day term for magic, and to practice magic effectively I feel we have to be aware of a few things…

1. The Universe has its own rhythms and timings.

2. That we are not inflicting our will on anybody else.

3. The Universe knows better than us.

4. Our thoughts and feelings actually come from the Universe and therefore we must be willing to surrender our will over to the Universe and be open to receive inspiration (spirit within).

5. Our own karmic path must be addressed in order to honour the above.

I feel that these things are easily overlooked and that is why we are getting what I call 'mega unaligned manifestations' or 'wonky wake up calls'!

There are so many stories of this type of thing happening. A client of mine wrote down that she wanted to meet someone between 5 foot 11 inches and 6 foot and she did, he had one leg shorter than the other!

A friend of mine was trying to sell her house so she visualized a 'sold' board in front of it – and got the sold board without the sale – effectively blocking the very thing she wanted!

Well the Universe seems like it has a 'wicked' sense of humour

– wicked as in cool as well as wicked! A high spiritual vibration involves incredible humour, this is how you can tell when you have really connected with a guide. Their great sense of humour is accompanied by a lack of ego. Spirit guides are called 'spirit guides' – not 'spirit answers' – for a reason. Guides don't exist to give us answers, they are here to guide us to discover the answers for ourselves, often through funny circumstances – circumstances that we may not find funny at the time and especially if we are attached to our ego. Our guides employ humour as the preferred teaching medium to encourage the development of detachment from our ego. Naturally this is where the crunch lies, for of course we are always attached to our ego – it's an innate part of being human. And actually we depend on the ego, just as much as the Universe depends on our ego as a vehicle to channel universal wisdom. The key is how to ensure our egos are working in alignment with the Universe and not against it.

So how do we do that? I will share with you a short meditation below. Once you are sitting comfortably and peacefully we can begin. (You may want to read this out onto a recorder and then play it back to yourself, the dots represent suggested pauses.)

## Opening to the Universe – Meditation

Close your eyes… take a lovely deep breath in and as you breathe out feel all of the day before now fall away, as if it is an overcoat falling off your shoulders and melting through the floor… now continue with your breathing for a few moments, really give yourself permission to let go of any residual tension… lovely… deep… relaxing breaths… imagine a screen inside your forehead… and see a number appear on it between 1-10… 1 being the least present, 10 being the most, you are not choosing or changing it, you are just noticing what is there with no judgment… we have to start with the truth or we block ourselves... if you feel the need to make your number higher then ask to be shown where the rest of your energy is... it could be with a person or a situation, or a multitude of them, so just call your energy back to you now with your breath... intend or see your energy returning to you now... feel where your energy clicks back into you and feel yourself becoming present and whole... bring your attention back up to your mind and see the word relax dissolve into tiny little droplets running down your head... releasing any tension in your temples... running down and releasing any tension in your jaw... these lovely drops of golden relaxation are melting away any tension held in the back of your neck and shoulders... relaxing and parting all the tiny muscles holding all the tension... it's melting away now as they run down your arms... your arms are feeling heavy, relaxed and tingly as the droplets run through your wrists and out through your fingers...

Now bring your attention back up to the screen of your mind and see the word calm... see the word calm dissolve into tiny droplets of calmness once again running down your temples, melting away any leftover tension... feel the droplets run down over your eyes... relaxing your eyelids... down over the bridge of your nose... over your lips... down the back of your head... over your ears, releasing any residual tension as they once again run down your jaw... relaxing and releasing any leftover tension... and into your heart... lovely deep breath in... and out... and relax your heart... feel the droplets run through your heart leaving a golden warmth and openness within as they run down into your torso... deep breath in... and out... and relax your torso... allow yourself to widen and sink into whatever is supporting you... allow yourself to feel supported... and let go... as these beautiful droplets of calmness and relaxation spread down into your hips... releasing, unlocking and relaxing your hips... and your thighs... feel your thighs relax and widen, sinking down, feeling heavier and heavier as they run down,

down, down through your knees, relax and release… as these beautiful droplets run down through your shins, relaxing and releasing… running down through your ankles, through your feet and out through your toes… leaving every part of you from your head to your toes beautifully calm and relaxed…

Now bring your attention back up and see a light emanating from the top of your head… expanding… growing… as this light grows bigger and bigger it becomes an amazing thousand petal lotus… unfolding… blossoming, blooming… further and further into infinity… see it connecting with the infinite light in the Universe, feel you and the Universe becoming one… you never were separate… just feel the dissolution of that illusion now as the atoms of your breath and being blend with the atoms of the energy of the Universe… we are made of the stars… we comprise of the very same prima material emerging from the Big Bang…. you and the matter of the cosmos are one… feel that now… feel yourself enveloped in the energy of your crown chakra… the gateway to the cosmos… as it grows larger and larger to envelop you now and just breathe into it… open up to all the wondrous possibility in the Universe… now have intent, have it clear in your mind, (if you can't find an intention just set your intention for inspiration to come to you over the next few days)… and just send out there into the Universe now with the words… "if this be for the greater good of all concerned this is what I wish to manifest, or if you dear Universe know better than I on this then let that be done"… send that message out to the Universe now… feel it release from within you and be sent out there like a supernova into the greater conscious… ask that you may become a channel for whatever is the Universe's will around this desire… and now start to let the feelings and visions fade… bringing your attention back to your breath and your body… breathe deeply, breathe the breath right down to your feet, breathe it out through your toes and wiggle your toes… breathe the breath right down your arms and out through your fingers… wiggling your fingers... lifting your arms up and stretching... yawning... breathing the breath right down into your heart and torso and breathing it out... feeling your body and giving yourself permission to move in whatever way your body needs to, in order to bring your presence back to the place you are in right now.

In undertaking this simple meditation you have effectively initiated your working relationship with the Universe, becoming a Co Creator and igniting your Youinverse! Once an intuitively felt connection with the Universe has happened, it's then time to fill the mind with a logical understanding of Co Creation. We do the process of connecting this way round because knowledge can sometimes block intuition.

The teachings of The Law of Attraction did wonders for waking us up to the realization that we all have ability to create our own reality. And despite all the hard work by wonderful writers who carefully compiled books to bring to consciousness the spiritual importance of the work involved, we humans still found ourselves governed by our demanding inner dwarves of Instant Gratification, Attachment, Addiction, Ego, Control, Fear and Greed. No matter how much we were told to 'let go' nobody was listening. Which, I am being informed is a natural part of the process. Now is the time for the next stage, we must go deeper.

The Law of Attraction was the first stage of our modern day society remembering and recalling the power within, and despite some great attempts at certain teachings around it, it seems like The Law of Attraction has become some sort of disembodied arm floating around today's culture, grabbing for all it can reach for. However, what's the point if you are just a disembodied arm? What can you really do with what you get anyway, except give it away again. And that's only if you are so called 'lucky enough' to get it. We have become like the sulky child who snaps "Soorrwwy!" just so she can get the sweetie (and since when were sweeties good for you anyway?). Or the person in love with love rather than you, who keeps telling you they love you. You can feel it, right? That silent but powerful demand for insatiable love, as if they want to rip your heart out and get momentary relief by giving themselves a temporary heart transplant with your very life blood. The fact it's not authentic or genuine doesn't make you want to respond in kind, does it? Do you think the Universe is any different? I am informed that this has no judgment attached to it, that it's a natural and an expected step in the process. We really do need to be very conscious. One woman when stressed shouted "I NEED A BREAK!" fell down the stairs and broke her leg. Another similar story is of someone I know, who whilst scrubbing, was cursing her neighbour for making the hall dirty. She stood up, slipped, and injured her leg so badly she was house bound for months. This lady works with mantras, she got the message about the power of thoughts and words. But have we? One can't help but wonder whether the Universe/Creation is trying to tell us something.

Back when I met my husband I was in a place in my life for perhaps the first time, where I truthfully did not want a relationship. I definitely didn't want to get married or have kids. So what happened? The most beautiful man I had ever met from the inside out arrived in my life, along with full custody of his ten-year-old daughter and a pretty consistent marriage proposal – that's what!

We have to remember that we don't know what is best for us, and thinking that we do may actually be a form of spiritual arrogance. Well, it's not the worst sin in the world to think that we know what's best for us, the real problem is when life gives us something that wasn't in our plan and we are too closed to listen. How are we ever going to receive what's in our best interest when in that self-absorbed state?

This reminds me of the joke about a man sitting on his roof during a flood. First a neighbour tries to help him to wade to safety. He says, "No, God will save me." Then a guy with a boat turns up to help. He says, "No, God will save me." And then a helicopter arrives, and he says, "No, it's okay, thanks – God will save me!"

Then he drowns in the flood, goes up to the Pearly Gates and gets an earful from St Peter. "You're not due here for thirty years, what happened?"

"Well," said the man, very upset, "I prayed to God and believed he'd save me, but he didn't."

"What are you talking about?" snaps St Peter. "We sent a neighbour, a boat and a helicopter. What were you expecting?"

The man had his own perception of what help looked like and because what arrived didn't fit with his ideology, he completely and literally missed the boat!

To me the modern day term 'The Law of Attraction' now means 'Paganism without the spirituality'. That may sound controversial and I am generalising, so please allow me a minute to explain...

The ancient religions of Paganism pre-date Christianity by many thousands of years, a practice where people understood and worked with (not against) the rhythms of life. They honoured certain times of the month and year, welcoming with grace and gratitude what was on offer at that time. Not invalidating the 'present' by hankering after something different. Their practice meant they knew things would come round at the right time.

Now doesn't some of that sound like the practices in 'The Law of Attraction' teachings? I'm sure you recognize the very powerful 'be grateful' teaching. Perhaps you have even practiced being grateful, and then got annoyed when it didn't work? Are we being truly grateful if we just practice it for a time to see if it will work for our agendas?

Now I am not saying that all Pagans were actually saints and we need to redeem them from the satanic labelling by Christianity. There were Pagans who used their knowledge for their own selfish ego, known as the dark side. The Law of Attraction also has a dark and light side, just like everything else.

To me 'The Law of Attraction' is really just a modern day term for 'Magic'. Somehow re-naming it makes it acceptable (or even cool) to be practising in society. If it was still called magic, would we be so comfortable openly talking and dabbling with it? Or would we feel that we might really need to know a lot more about what we are doing before practicing it?

There are a lot of reasons why in the past magic was kept underground, and not just because of being driven there by the condemnation of the Roman Catholic Church. Essentially The Law of Attraction has brought magic above ground. It has removed some of the fears and taboos of practising magic and made it socially acceptable. A fantastic occurrence and a necessary step in evolutionary consciousness. However, that necessary step meant that a lot of us were the equivalent of curious and excited children playing around with real magic wands. Can you imagine the havoc? If you have seen the Disney classic *The Sorcerer's Apprentice* ask yourself what it reminds you of.

As I am writing this, my thoughts turn to my first book in this series. How that too was all about understanding and respecting the rhythms of life by using the ancient art of Tarot, busting through the fears and misunderstandings around such an ancient and misjudged practice. Now I feel my guides are working with me to do the same thing with Co Creation/The Law of Attraction or 'Magic'.

Whilst writing the last few paragraphs, it has struck me how as a species right now we are collectively vibrating as the archetypes of The Fool and The Magician within the Tarot. The Fool is the child with the magic wand. Oblivious to the danger he's in. He has a stick slung over his shoulder, so carelessly, to carry his satchel of possessions, but the stick is really his magic wand. He is so unaware that it is coloured black to signify being kept in the dark. The Fool is the baby of the Tarot. He represents entering a whole new cycle of evolution, unaware of the power he holds. So if he is the newborn, how did he get that bit of baggage?

Well that's called karma, something he is completely unaware of. So off he goes through life causing havoc as his magic wand fires off unconsciously in all directions behind him, through his karmic baggage. During the time that The Law of Attraction sprang up, we danced between the archetype of The Fool and the beginning stages of the very next archetype – The Magician.

The less a Magician knows the more likely he is to be consumed by his passions. He risks being eaten up by his own ego, represented by his red cloak and his association with the number one. Me first, I win, etc. The more a Magician learns, the more likely he is able to understand the need to work with the rhythms of nature. He not only understands that what goes around comes around, but he vibrates to this tune. Ultimately once he transcends his ego centredness, he embraces and embodies the message that there actually is no other way to operate except for the highest good of all concerned. In the Tarot, The Magician often has an infinity symbol hovering above his head representing the strong, sacred, never-ending flow of karma: the message being that what you put out, you get back. His white robe represents light, information and consciousness, as does his upright stance.

We are moving into matriarchal times, which are the next two archetypes in the natural order of the Tarot (The High Priestess and The Empress), but we cannot get there until we have moved fully through The Magician. The more a Magician knows, the more he realizes he is a Co Creator, a channel, like an aerial for a radio or TV. Correctly aligned he will pick up and tune into the broadcast the Universe is constantly transmitting. The Universe needs his physicality to make this manifest and The Magician in turn is interdependent upon the Universe in order to evolve. The Co Creation ignites his Youniverse. His purpose is to pick up the communication from the Universe satellite and manifest it here on Earth. He is a truly aligned Co Creator.

The younger Magician sees this communication as his own thoughts, feelings, wants and needs. His ego takes over and plays Chinese whispers with him, ignites his desire and causes attachment. He then sets out to create and manifest the things he feels he needs to attain for himself. As this happens, the natural order of Creation becomes unbalanced, the message he has broadcast through his magic wand/aerial is "You must be out for what you can get. Think of number one, no one else will – survival of the fittest." Society picks up on it and starts to resonate from LACK ( L = Losing, A = Attaining, C = Chaos, K = Keeping) and FEAR (F = False, E = Expectations, A = Appearing R = Real) creating a culture of the "I win, you lose" mentality, which in turn breeds a general social malaise of distressed feelings of separation… And that is the cause of the disembodied arm, endlessly, blindly grab-grab-grabbing.

The older Magician knows his thoughts and feelings are not his own. He has learnt that they come from somewhere else before he identified with them. They are being downloaded (channelled) through him to serve a higher purpose. He realizes the importance of non-attachment, and remaining conscious enough to make sure his own agenda does not interfere. He knows he is a channel for a higher purpose. (As I write this, a line is playing from my music shuffle – "Round here we always stand up straight. Round here something radiates…" – Counting Crows.)

I was granted a poignant learning experience in the process of getting The *Transformational Truth of Tarot* published. It proved to be an eighteen-month long journey of recurring misalignment! I had become full of fear, stressed around losing control, and I came to realize that there was absolutely no need for my fear and stress. I had already been offered a contract, but my lack of trust meant I held out to see if there was anything else around. The longer I held out and the more I searched, the more unaligned I became. The Hanged Man in the Tarot (place of being stuck until you realize what you are hung up on and detach yourself) began to haunt me, not just in the readings I was doing, but also in the manifestation of my dreams and my waking life too. A busker had even taken a pitch outside the shop I was reading in. He would hang himself upside down just like The Hanged Man and start playing a guitar (representing playing around). Or I would walk down Neal Street and often see another busker, standing on his head with a bucket on it (representing not being able to see). But still I did not click. I did figure after six months and a bucket load (ha!) of synchronicities that I should sign the contract. So I did, expecting everything to come back up to speed thus freeing myself of The Hanged Man. But alas, the haunting continued. A year later, I was meditating and I became aware of The Hanged Man's presence behind me in the meditation – "God! Not a minute's peace!" I thought, and in utter frustration turned round and shouted at him, "WHAT?"

"Tiffany, you are so hung up on the timing of this book, and it's not yours. It was gifted to you, through you. What makes you think you have the divine right on the timing?"

I was gobsmacked! Especially as I am a Leo – our core lesson is to remember that we don't create it all!

"Well, okay then, I hand it over gladly, you have the responsibility, thank God! That feel's amazing! WOW! Blissssssssssss…" I remember thinking.

But the most amazing thing was yet to come, I got home to an email from the publisher saying they wanted it in for printing the very next week, I looked at the time it was sent – and yes the very time I let go!

It was all hands on deck from that very moment on. However, that meant that I had to spend the week reading and re-reading my book, and that week I just happened to be running a retreat, which also required all hands on deck. This meant that in the rush certain typos were missed and it was now too late to rectify.

I started to get back in Hanged Man mode as soon as I started to fear the judgments I was sure would come in. But I realized once again that I was worrying about something I had no control over, and I unattached myself quickly.

I stopped feeling attached to my ambitions for *The Transformational Truth of Tarot*. I love the book, it has its own life, it goes on its own travels and sometimes I will hear of news of what it is up to and it makes me smile. It's like getting postcards from it as it travels the globe and it amazes me with what it gets up to. I love that it is out there meeting, connecting and having a great time with so many people, and all without me of course! How could it do so well with me controlling its course when it could have the Universe as a guide?

One day, four months after it was published, a friend said, "Congratulations on the book, Tiffany!"

"Erm, are you okay? Am I okay? Are you senile? Or am I experiencing *déjà vu*? I'm sure you said this to me four months ago."

"Don't you know?"

"Know what?"

"It won an award!"

Well I leapt up and flung my arms around my friend – trouble was, I was wearing a tight denim skirt with poppers down the front and ... whoops! Suddenly no skirt! Talk about luck making itself – I did know it had been entered, but I hadn't entered it – someone else had. Nor was I the first one to find out it had won; I had been the channel for it, and that's it. By letting that communication go out into the world with no attachment, I was allowing it to do its own thing...

## Questions to Ask 1 = Self

Write your answers below in pencil so you can go back to this in a few months and see where you were, erase your history making room for your development – magic in itself, words aren't known as 'spelling' for no reason. Your Youniverse needs you to be brutally honest here, so go for it!

- Do you practice The Law of Attraction or Magic?

- Why?

- What do you feel about the disembodied arm analogy? Do you see that in any area of your life? If so what areas? And what can you do to work through this? If you don't know the answer, don't worry just come back to this question later. Your subconscious will work on it as you keep reading and you will get 'aha' moments sooner or later.

- Do you feel like a baby with a magic wand? How does that feel to you? Scary, or exciting? What would you point your wand at and why? Is this coming from ego, or a pure channel for the highest good of everyone?

- Do you feel like a sulky child saying "sowrry" just to get the sweetie in any area of your life? If so which ones?

- Do you feel like a young magician, aware of your power, but not yet able to resist using it in the hope you can bend others wills to your own? Is there a particular area in your life where this behaviour is more pronounced? If so what could you do to work on your alignment?

- Do you feel like a mature magician, aware that your power is a Co Creative power in alignment with the Universe? Do you know that you must stand up straight and not get pulled around by your own wants, desires and ego in order to stay on track and allow your life to blossom? Is there a particular area in your life that struggles with this? If so what is it? And how can you help yourself? Come back to this question later if you don't know the answer yet.

- Are you attached to something being a certain way? If so what is it? Why are you so sure it has to be that way? How is that making you feel? Entertain how you might feel if you let it go.

- Are you the lover or mother that just says I love you because you want to hear it in return? If so, how is that working for you?

So what is luck anyway? A question of perception? Maybe it is how we perceive ourselves, or how our own circumstances are perceived by others. My journey of learning with luck was very connected to my journey with Lauren. In those four months she was here, the amount of so called luck, or 'unluck' – depending on the perception, was intense…

The day the hospital discharged her with the words, "There is no point keeping her here, there is nothing more we can do, take her home, we have written do not resuscitate on her notes," I walked across the hospital car park with her tucked up in her carry car seat for the first ever time, and a tall, gaunt looking lady walked towards me. She looked hauntingly at Lauren, her presence stopping me in my tracks. Turning her eyes to me, they bore into mine as she said the words… "You don't know how lucky you are."

In that very moment I vowed never to say that phrase to anyone and I never have. I spent a lot of time wondering why that encounter happened; I believed I knew how lucky I was. Some people may say I was terribly unlucky – but that's not how I saw it. I felt incredibly blessed to have an incredible soul like Lauren enter my life and tear my heart open so I may truly start living. I recognized that call and wished to embrace the experience with the recognition of the sacredness this encounter held. Yet the lady's words struck me with the same force as a physical blow. All I could do was bite my tongue and swallow the large, hard lump that appeared in my throat from nowhere. But looking back perhaps she was the equivalent of an angel. Just making sure I didn't slip, or forget. And believe me I didn't.

"Home, James" it was for Christmas 1997 as we motored our way home for the first time as a new family of three. I guess in that way the NHS became my Father Christmas. Lauren appeared to go from strength to strength. Declared deaf in hospital, at home she developed A1 hearing. We were told she would never smile or interact with us, but at home she did just that. She was so happy to be home, so much so that the power of her happiness began to defy what the hospitals were telling us and we began to wonder if she was such a miracle that she would out do her prognosis too. But come February 1998 Lauren began to slip into heart failure, her whole body would heave with each and every breath, her tiny body just caught up to newborn baby weight (but only due to water retention) was working so very hard to stay with us. Nevertheless her smile remained. Lauren's heart was the most affected organ by the syndrome, two huge holes and a malfunctioning aorta. The hospital told me she was going into heart failure and needed to be admitted – she never left. Well not in her body with spirit intact. But she did leave, in stages. The first stage was as soon as she was admitted. Her happiness left. I saw it happen, the very moment they plugged her up to the machines and remarked astoundingly that no baby could possibly be alive with oxygen saturates of 27 and a heart rate of 248 beats a minute.

Her smile left, replaced only by inconsolable crying and sporadic fitting. One of these fits caused the onset of pneumonia, and from that moment on they were hunting all over her tiny deteriorating body trying so hard to administer cannulas of morphine with the intention of calming her distressed body and mind. In defiance her veins would collapse – but the chase continued until she was black and blue all over. This sorry saga lasted a whole fortnight until life support was all that was left. The doctor came in and said that there was no point keeping her on life support, she would never come off. They had managed to find a vein to administer morphine and they wanted permission to administer the highest legal dose they could, which would speed up the process.

And…

We gave it.

They brought her back to us, and from that moment on she did not leave our arms. During the afternoon, there were times she gained sudden consciousness. Her whole body looked like it was going through a mix of shock and fear, this would last a handful of seconds only and thankfully she would soon drift back off into some kind of what felt a relatively peaceful state. This was the second stage; she had arrived at a land between pain and peace.

At 19:20 on 17th March 1998 (St Patrick's day) I felt her spirit come away from her utterly exhausted body and my arms. With her last breath, I felt her soul releasing from the body we named Lauren Etienne, fly up to the hospital ceiling and out of the window into the evening sky. Leaving us all with the deepest sense of peace we had ever felt, it was astounding. Here we were in a room that only minutes before had been filled with such upset and fear in all of us, including Lauren. Now we were in a place where reality said, that's it, bottom line. The day I had dreaded finally arrived and it said to me, "Here I am, the day where you start learning how to live without your baby girl." Yet the feeling of peace she left immediately following her passing is something I will never forget.

Even so, I rose in a state of shock and fear of the peace. Needing to keep busy, I said, "Right, I am going to ring round and let everyone know." And I walked out the room. Walking down the hospital corridor, I came across a ward full of broken nurses trying to hide their tears from me. It's funny how people do that isn't it? Their tears for my daughter went a long way to healing the first bits of pain, yet society had conditioned them to hide from me. For me it was a validation that she wasn't just an NHS number, it was a recognition of the special child she was. Little was I to know just how many people's lives she had touched. This was just the beginning. At the time of Lauren's funeral I don't think I had ever seen a church so full, nor since, even though she had only been around four months. I was in a daze in those days, all I remember is an absolute sea of heads and a constantly jammed letterbox full of cards and notes from people I had never met, who she had never met, expressing how just knowing about her had touched them. The ripples of Lauren I had only seen in my immediate environment, was only one minute drop of her presence and purpose.

Back to the hospital, and the moment I saw the nurses embarrassed because I had seen their tears. I turned on the spot and walked in the opposite direction, literally bumping into a new father, who said to me, "I've just seen your daughter, she is looking so well!" In fact, he wasn't the only one, and this happened another two or three times between that evening and the morning we left. These were people I didn't even know, I hadn't registered them previously and now they were coming up to me telling me how well my daughter was doing. This, at a time when I hadn't even managed to inform all my friends and family that she had passed, felt like quite a confusing, painful, awkward and (unlucky) repetitive experience.

The morning we left the hospital, the nurse gave me a card that my best friend had sent to Lauren. Inside it said, "Stay strong and look after your mummy". The stamp on the envelope said, "Don't forget Mother's Day this Sunday". At that time in my life I nearly slipped again. I perceived all those synchronicities as cruel twists of a salted blade on one hell of a sharpened unlucky knife. But my love for Lauren meant there was no way I was going to invalidate all she had been through; to come here to teach me that life was a gift, so I hung on and vowed to learn just how to start doing life justice and as the years went on the pain got less as the understandings grew. Through a visitation that I will speak about later, I realized that perhaps these people had really seen Lauren and that they were telling me how well she was – what seemed cruel was actually my perception, just like the encounter with the lady in the car park, "lady luck" had paid me a visit, a reminder to stay on the path – just how fortunate was that?

My life has been full of very strange happenings since I was born, but they would be better described as psychic phenomena (look out for another book). My first remembrance of experiencing what I would term strictly as 'synchronicity' was with Lauren, when I was six weeks pregnant and the complete stranger stopped me in the street to tell me her birth date. That was now seventeen years ago and the strength of synchronicity (magic) in my life that I experience on a regular basis, is beyond belief sometimes. Looking back I wonder if Lauren bought with her that strong gift of synchronicity/magic. But I get the answer that it was about so much more than that. Lauren bought with her the opportunity for me to open or close. To learn how to work with karma in a way that turns it into luck or magic, and creates our own Youniverse. The synchronicities are merely an outer reflection.

I am being told that this book is far more than one book on one subject. It's being written to heal and transform individual and collective pain found within the Earth, the collective and us as individuals, by looking at how to work with our individual and collective karma and turn it into luck and Co Creative magic.

To give you an idea of how I see this manifesting, it's time for me to share with you how my daughter (who is one of my strongest guides) works. Through doing so, your own *Transformational Truth of You* may happen. But before I do that there is a little exercise for you to reflect with below. The point system in it may be useful to you, or it may not. You may have your own to think about and design from your own set of values. All exercises in this book are only suggestions and come from a place of offering something that may be useful, they are not meant as a yardstick or judgment, it's for you to find your own, what is below is just an example.

So if you are up for it I suggest that you run your eyes over the questions below and rate yourself truthfully between one and ten. Ten being 'I strongly agree' and one being 'I completely disagree'.

## Taking a Graceful Measure

1. I see life as a gift the majority of the time.

2. When something upsetting happens I realize it's my perception of it that's the problem, and it's just that I don't understand it yet.

3. I trust that life is working for my highest good – even when it doesn't feel like it.

4. In fact when it doesn't feel like it, I trust it more.

5. I understand that for real blossoming to occur in our lives we need to keep working on ourselves.

6. And I am *actively committed* to my own inner development and understanding.

7. I understand that in order for things to happen I need to be open.

8. I manage to walk through this life open – and not just when it's easy.

9. I believe that I have been given a set of ingredients in life and no matter what they are, I can make a masterpiece from them, once I accept them for what they are.

10. I believe there is a reason for everything – even if I can't see what it is.

SCORING

Even more important than your score, is whether you did this honestly, and if so which question triggered you? That very trigger is a clue on where to start on your next step of development.

0–25

Pick a perception from the above list that you feel you can start with and make a commitment to practice that for the next month; best to start with the 'I understand' ones, rather than the 'commit' ones – be gentle on yourself. Do this, not in the hope of seeing your external life shifting in that time, but just to see how you feel in yourself. Practice adding a perception each month, building up step by step. You could also keep a journal in order to track how your journey is doing, and to track any synchronicities that start occurring to show you that the Universe is hearing you and commending you. BUT also know that it is important to really keep the focus on yourself; synchronicity increases in our lives the more open we get. Don't be downhearted if it isn't yet occurring. See the fact that there is no synchronicity as a sign that you need to bring the attention back to yourself more first.

25–50

It sounds as if you've been through the mill and are starting to realize the importance on shifting your perception – it may be helpful to look over how far you have already come, perhaps start a journal and write down all the things in your life that you have achieved – be it large or small. You might be the only one who knew about these achievements, or perhaps these are things you haven't seen in yourself but you have received compliments on. Take a look at the statements again and assess where you are at now – do you need to work more on practicing understanding, or is it time to step up your commitment? Choose a perception and practice it for three weeks. Record in your journal your feelings throughout that time and any happenings that seem important.

50- 75

It seems like you have the understanding and the practice in place. It's just about strengthening that now. Ask yourself what you could do to help yourself with that? Were there any perceptions above that you particularly struggled with? If so, why? This shows your next step, put it into practice, and as you do keep a journal to see how that is manifesting for you – firstly on the inside, your thoughts, feelings, inspirations, etc.

75–100

Firstly if you got towards 100 I would firstly ask you if you are being really honest – only because if you aren't you will block yourself. So firstly go back and really see if you are. If you have done that, and you still get the same score or higher, then only you will know which ones were your weakest points to start working on in order to strengthen your channel further.

# Chapter 3

# Temperance

## Sourcing Messages from the Past for the Future

*Has it ever occurred to you that one hundred pianos all tuned to the same fork are automatically tuned to each other? They are of one accord by being tuned, not to each other, but to another standard to which each one must individually bow. So one hundred worshipers met together, each one looking away to Christ, are in heart nearer to each other than they could possibly be, were they to become 'unity' conscious and turn their eyes away from God to strive for closer fellowship.*
– A.W Towzer

My daughter is beyond a doubt one of the greatest guides I have, and I am amazingly blessed to have a guide incarnate with me for a short while in order to show me one of the biggest lessons I really had to learn. If she hadn't done that I do think the chances of me not being on the planet would be relatively high by now. Each and every day since Lauren was conceived my sense of purpose has only ever grown. Looking back over the years, I have seen how my daughter goes out of her way to say hello, especially around the anniversary of her passing.

It was very clear that she was around for the first six months after her death. We moved away from my family and friends the very day after her funeral, another seemingly cruel twist. Being an army family we were due our first posting. The army had changed the location especially to suit Lauren's needs, a special flat close to a hospital that knew about her. The other seemingly cruel twist was that it was the same hospital she was transferred to and never left. She made it to about five miles away from her new home, and now we were arriving at the new home, without her.

Somewhere completely new for the first time in my life, family and friends no longer just down the road. Only the hospital my daughter had passed in for company like a haunting monument reminding me – not that I needed reminding. Doing my 'must keep busy' thing again, I found work almost immediately and made new friends. At first, they did not know about Lauren and when they came round to our place they would all remark how it smelt of babies. When Lauren was here I used to spend as much time as possible taking in her scent. I could keep her photos, videos, toys and clothes. But her smell was something that gave me an indescribable amount of comfort, and I couldn't bear the thought of there being a day when it would fade.

I would listen to a tape of her songs regularly, yes back in the tape days! Quite often the grief and sounds of music would have me staring emptily out the window until some type of trance would come in and give me a brief sense of peace. One particular afternoon the trance was broken by hearing the tape stop and rewind itself after a song. I was amazed as I heard how it had rewound itself and stopped to play the song again! In a lucid state I turned around and saw her – fitting perfectly across the cushion of the armchair, just where she always liked to be. Looking once again so happy, just like she used to. The vision lasted about 20 seconds and filled me with utter bliss. You could argue that grief does some funny things. But when other people witness these things, then how do you explain it? Only I witnessed that one but it got me thinking, why were those people coming up to me saying, 'I've just seen your daughter, and she looks so great!" just after her passing? Perhaps it wasn't a cruel misunderstanding after all. Perhaps that was just my interpretation.

The signs of Lauren being around began to fade after six months, but still, around anniversary time, happenings occurred.

In the first few years I still had her toys around me and friends would notice the musical ones would start to play a few notes. On the time of the third year anniversary I heard a smack as something crashed to the floor. I looked to find the 3D cross cut picture of Lauren's nursery lying face down. When I picked it up the round gold ring that acted as a picture frame in the installation had jammed itself on the doll's head that represented her and become a halo!

When she was here there were times I would have her in my arms, thinking she was asleep I would be drifting off, and then all of a sudden an incredibly strong feeling of love would wake me. I would turn to see her beautiful big brown eyes sending the love right into my soul, carried in with a stunningly consistent smile, something we were told she wouldn't be capable of due to the lack of a corpus callosum (the centre in the brain responsible for co-ordination). The best memory of this was during the classical singing part of the film *The Fifth Element*. I was stirred from my sleep by the sounds of the beautiful vocal chords, yes, but more than that, by a deep incredible feeling of love being sent right into the heart of my very being. I opened my eyes to see Lauren looking deep into mine with the most incredible smile on her face. I knew that moment would be my most cherished memory.

Around the time of her anniversary three years ago a dear friend said one of his favourite films was on TV and did I want to watch it? Yes, *The Fifth Element*! I relayed the above story to him and then said let's turn it on and see if it's at that very scene, we did, it was – his turn to be gobsmacked!

The *Fifth Element* film feels linked to Lauren. So let's look at this:

- The four elements are earth, air, fire and water and the fifth is spirit.

- Lauren's Sagittarian birth date means she resonated with Temperance in Tarot, which is trump number 14 (1+4 elements = 5th element).

- In numerology Lauren's birth date makes her a number seven, 24/11/1997 (2+4+1+1+1+9+9+7 = 34 3+4 = 7) like me 11/8/77 (1+1+8+1+9+7+7 = 34 3+4 = 7) So if you put us together, 2x7 = 14, 1+4 = 5 and round we go back to The Fifth Element again.

It would be best to keep those points in mind for now, as we will come back to them later on in the story…

On her fifteenth anniversary I had just begun giving readings on TV. I met a friend for a drink afterwards. As we were leaving she said to me, "I have been thinking of you today." I said, "Yes, today is the first anniversary where I haven't had time to buy her flowers. I buy baby pink carnations every year and throw them into the water, where her ashes are; but it's too late now." Just as I finished that very sentence we turned a corner to leave the bar and by the door there was a gigantic floral display, full of pink flowers for sale – in a bar!? The pink flowers were so many it was quite an impact; we looked through the huge pink display for baby pink carnations, one bunch hiding humbly below. The lady came along and told us that the florist section was shut. My friend was about to protest and I stopped her to say that it was okay. I was not to buy them; this was Lauren, telling me this was for me that year. And I realized I got it. Really got it. There are no cruel twists in the Universe, only perceptions.

However perhaps the most relevant teaching to this book is the anniversary message that happened in 2011…

A few days before her anniversary I dreamt of a musical jewellery box playing "Try" by Nelly Furtado. It felt enigmatic, but I didn't give it any more thought. Logging on to the computer I found an email from a new student I had met the day before, apologising for being so distracted throughout the class. She explained that she was taken by the presence of a baby girl who was telling her that I was her mother, and that she was trying to communicate with me through my dreams.

Just writing this now brings the tingles back all over my body.

I Googled the lyrics to "Try" straight away, and urge you to look them up to see the message I received.

I read it over and over again, the words blurred on the screen through the tears welling up in my eyes sporadically falling down my face, and into my grateful heart.

The story is below; it is full of numerology, astrology and archetypes. If it was ever to be made into a film it would probably be one of those films that you would need to watch a few times to get it all, so go through the chapter not worrying about anything you might not consciously get. Whatever your conscious clicks with at this moment in time is what is meant for you now, and if you ever come back to read it again I am sure you will pick up on a different aspect, relevant for you then.

## The Beginning Message

A couple of days after the "Try" message I was regressing a lady, she was reliving a life as one of the most powerful Nazis of the Second World War. It may be important to mention that she already felt she was this person through a series of events, and we were doing this to see if she was right. She was horrified at the thought that she may have been Heydrich. The lady began talking in a German accent and appeared so very pale. After accessing the life she went into the between life state where she saw a mass amount of souls returning to the light. She was overcome with pain and her guides were telling her it was just a necessary step. She was arguing with them, saying how can they say that? A bit of pain for growth may be necessary, but this amount was debilitating. However, that very thought seemed to be part of the next step as she went on to tell me about her life selection as the lady she is today, why she is in the career she is and how her path is all about healing a pain blockage in the Earth. I asked her if her location was correct for this, and she told me that her location – Cornwall (as well as Glastonbury) is the heart chakra of the world. That Cornwall is in particular the aorta (the main problem with Lauren's heart) and that is why it's Cornwall's job to pump, the mining system just a mere outward manifestation of this energy. She spoke of an energy grid in the Earth being blocked by pain, in particular the sheer amount of pain from the two world wars. That this pain blockage is the reason that the shift the Earth is going through now is feeling so traumatic. She said that if people gathered in Cornwall with love, meditation and peace it would help heal the blockage and shift to be more peaceful.

I sat on the fence with this for a while… But not for long

## Message Two

The night after, my husband and I watched a film recommended to us called *Pay It Forward* in which a teacher sets an assignment to his class to think of something to change the world. My husband needed to go into the kitchen so he paused it and walked out the room, completely unaware of the scene he had paused it on. I, however, was sitting there with it staring me in the face for about five minutes. The scene was of a close up of the blackboard, upon which the teacher had written, "Think of something to change the world and put it into action". He returned oblivious and we continued to watch.

In the film a boy changed the world by a simple but profound idea; instead of paying a favour back, the person he did the favour for was to pay it forward to three others and so on. By the end of the film he was disheartened. In his perception he had failed. He could not see the change happening in the immediate environment. The ripples however lived on, unlike him.

I went incredibly quiet. My husband asked me why I thought the writer had killed the boy off and my thoughts were already there. I felt that the shorter a life, the more intense the impact; they have to do their thing in a very short space of time. The author had to kill the boy in order to show the standing legacies we leave behind, the power of a life filled in line with our purpose. It may not have been so well demonstrated all the time he was alive – just as I feel with Lauren.

Then I began to think, what if there is still more to be done from Lauren's life? What if I haven't got the whole message?

## Message Three

The third day I end up having another client for regression. As they go through the regression it becomes evident that they are a German from World War I. I now wonder what is going on, realizing that I had never had a client regress to either of the world war periods before, let alone two, covering the two, two days apart.

- I started to feel that the number 11 has great significance in all of this, which I tell to my husband. And he informed me that he thought the Second World War finished at 11:11 on the 11th – three pairs of one, reminding me of triple chromosomes Lauren had. I researched it to find that it was the First World War that finished on the 11th of 11th at 11am. I then realize that the First World War and Second World War are written with one Roman numeral and then two Roman numerals (WWI and WWII) looking like 1:11.

- In the Tarot, 1 is about commencement, and 11 Justice – so putting them together you get commencement of justice – commencement of Justice often involves a long period of perceived injustice. I begin to ask myself (perhaps controversially) if the world wars were actually a commencement of Justice that has been waiting for 2011 to put right (2nd chance [0 – opportunity] at 11?).

- The number 1 is also about the power of the channel in the self, (like we spoke about with The Magician earlier) and 11 is also the number for service, so if you put 1 together with 11 you get the two extremes of self and service (Youniverse).

- The addition of triple 1 gets the result of three, an odd number signifying unstable periods as things grow, also representing birth (from two comes a third). The patterns of putting 1s together for pairs or triplicates, triggers thoughts of Lauren's chromosomes. Her pair (11) splitting 'incorrectly' to get a single 1, resulting in a third chromosome, and then splitting incorrectly again to get a balance (11).

- The next day happened to be the date of the Japanese Tsunami – date 11/3/11.

- Astrologically speaking, at the time of the Tsunami the Asteroid Pallas (also looking like 11 in how it is spelt) moved into Aquarius, which is the 11th sign of the zodiac in the 11th house (the sign and house are both about evolution and group consciousness) for 11 months (again three pairs of 1 – like the chromosomes). Aquarius is actually also Pallas, who is connected to Apollo (Athena, Warrior Goddess of Justice). I think I must reiterate here that in the Tarot, the 11th card is Justice.

With each day that turns, I feel more and more, like the Earth is going through a new birth. One where we have to stand up straight (like 11) and be aligned channels for the Universe. I feel it is more important than ever before to get to know 1 = self and our purpose, to wake up to the realisation of the importance of being true to 1 = self. In order to do that we must wake up to what is going on within us and realize we are Co Creative channels for divinity here on Earth.

Everyone has been born with a light to shine, a gift to give, a purpose to fill. But with mass employment in our society, the ability to be 1 = self has become increasingly blocked, just like the pain blockage in the Earth. We are a micro of the macro. We have wielded to others' wills (just like people did with Hitler) resulting in a blockage of our own, this is no longer being allowed. Hence we find ourselves in a worldly recession, which just keeps digging deeper, and as it does, more and more people are being expelled from others' wills and forced to follow their own. The time is now to discover what our gifts are and let them shine, that way we become a channel, upright like 11 and we begin to do the world (and ourselves) justice.

## Message Four

I spoke to a friend about this theme of new birth and living our truth and as we finish she emailed me to say that we stopped talking at 11:11. I didn't even bring up the subject of 11 with her. I began thinking about these numbers again; I thought about my birthday, which that year was 11/08/11. Eight in the Tarot is the Strength card, but it wasn't always. Three years before the First World War began in 1914 (note the presence of 14 1+4 (elements) = 5 = spirit; Lauren would have been 14 in 2011, just note this for now); in 1911 (note the three 1s) a member of the secret order of The Golden Dawn, Mr Arthur Edward Waite swapped Justice (which was the 8th card) with the 11th card, Strength. Because real strength is something fluid and never ending just like the symbol of infinity, the symbol that looks like 8, which is present on the number 1 card The Magician. Justice was more upright, like pillars of society, 11.

The Mayan calendar began on my birthday back in 3114 BC (I look good for my age)! Look again at the presence of 3, 1 and 14. I was born at 11:13 pm, again we have the three ones and one three. I then add up my birthday and get fourteen – the age Lauren was at the time, adding 1 and 4 equalling The Fifth Element.

Remember the fourteenth card of the Tarot is Temperance. Temperance is Sagittarius – just like Lauren. Temperance in Greek mythology is the Goddess Iris, The Goddess of the Rainbow (Arco Iris), who oversees the passing of souls from our world to whatever world is next appropriate for them. This triggers my memory of the lady talking about the mass of souls passing over from the world wars, when she was under regression.

Back to the film *The Fifth Element*, The Fifth Element (who is an alien) nearly gives up on humanity and loses the will to live when she sees footage of the world wars. Bruce Willis (who I guess is her equivalent of a Twin Flame in today's terminology) had been told that she is more fragile than she seems and that she will need his support and love to survive. He needed to master the ability to re-open his own heart (which had been closed by a pain blockage in him) in order to save himself, The Fifth Element and the Earth. Of course, he manages it with seconds to spare. He opens his heart, his love for her restores her faith in love and humanity reviving her will to live. The light bursts out from their hearts, sending a mass stream of light up from the Earth into the core of the evil entity that was threatening the Earth (the government had previously tried to kill it with war and it only kept regrouping with more strength). By releasing the pain blockage in the their hearts, hers caused by war, his by loss, they align spirit and physicality to Co Create a power of spiritual and physical love strong enough to overcome anything.

What with the regressions, *The Fifth Element*, Temperance, the paused scene from the film *Paying It forward* ("think of something to change the world and put it into action" and the boy who starts to do that and then dies, but the healing lives on through his spirit), and what with the message brought to me both through my dream and through a student prompting me to look up the uncanny lyrics to "Try", I begin to wonder if this is part of Lauren's work. Perhaps there is even a backlog of souls still waiting to pass from the world wars? Either way, I started to feel Lauren was working with me to aid the peaceful transition and healing of the Earth and, as if it was being sent as confirmation, I started to see 111 everywhere, the meaning of which is powerful channelling and fast manifestations, not of your own desires, but that of the Universe.

## Message Five

I was sitting in meditation with two selenite crystal wands, one in each hand, and I found myself becoming the dancer in The World card. The World card pictures the final step of evolution on the Soul's journey. The Wand in Tarot is a channel for the consciousness of creation; as spoken about previously when it is black it represents unconsciousness, and when white consciousness. Throughout the Tarot there is a repetitive theme of one black wand and one white wand (11). In The World card the dancer twirls two white wands (just like I was holding the two white selenite wands in my meditation) showing that evolution has taken place resulting in complete enlightenment and consciousness. The World card is number 20, the number 11 is pictured in the card by the two wands and the **"Laurel"** wreath representing the world looks like a zero, making up 2011. Inside the wreath the two wands (looking like 11) are twirling around, representing fluid, never ending strength. Is this the picture of the pole shift I began to wonder?

## Message Six

I heard that Japan is the crown chakra of the world, and I researched it, finding a number of sources that believe it is, alongside Hawaii and a number of other places. Japan fits more for me being a Reiki teacher as Reiki is all about the crown chakra. So if it is, it seems like the world has gone through a huge Kundalini awakening right from the root chakra down in Uluru, Australia. The grand meridian of the world known as the Rainbow Serpent (Laurel wreath in The World card) begins at Uluru, and the highest point of the meridian (energy line) is under St Michael's Mount, which is near where I live in Cornwall, on the other side of Mount's bay, opposite me.

St Michael's Mount is a place I used to see regularly in my dreams before I knew it was the mount. Dreams of huge tidal waves, seas that parted (St Michael's Mount has a path to the shore when the tide is low) and a man in a chariot pulled by two horses galloping through. Lauren and I are both number sevens numerologically speaking; the seventh card in the Tarot is The Chariot. The Chariot is pulled by two horses, one black and one white – being Sagittarian she is represented by half man, half horse.

St Michael's Mount is also the point where the major ley lines of Michael and Mary cross, as well as the line of Apollo Athena (three lines – 111); which takes me back round to Pallas, what with it being literally the pinnacle of the rainbow serpent pumping the energy around the world. Does this mean that Cornwall is indeed the heart pump of the world, the Aorta? If Japan is the crown then perhaps the Tsunami represented some kind of worldly Kundalini awakening?

Synchronistically speaking, I came back to refine this chapter in February 2014 and Cornwall was being hit by a severe storm that began early in the month and carried on to mid-month. Seventy-five foot waves were recorded off the coast of Mount's bay – thankfully they didn't come in that high, but the waves were still huge enough to cause complete devastation of homes, railways and landmarks that had stood for hundreds if not thousands of years.

## Message Seven

Now I knew I had to act – I had to help the lady who brought through this communication from her past life experience as Heydrich. When I tell the lady, she says she had a dream about masses gathering in white (like Temperance) – at St Michael's Mount. The Temperance card in the Rider Waite deck looks like a painting of St Michael's Mount. At this realization I start to see the cells of the Earth reforming to make two wrongs a right (the two world wars of I and of I and II) but the blockage in the aorta is an almighty challenge to heal, just like in Lauren's experience.

Did a syndrome surface in the world during World War I and II (triple chromosome) just like Lauren's chromosomes that split incorrectly again, which actually restored some cells into the correct alignment (11:11) but some were left 1:11. Here two wrongs almost made a right but it couldn't rectify the damage in the past, and may have been the cause of more misunderstandings and therefore more pain. Is this what happened in World War II (and is it an accident that Hitler's DNA contains Jewish DNA)?

Did we see Earth have an attempt at rectification in the Tsunami of 11/3/11?

So, like the boy in the film. I tried to arrange a world-healing event, where people gathered all at the same time at energy spots across the world to channel love and healing into the Earth. People downloaded the MP3 and we all listened and linked in together through knowing we were all on the same journey, the power of collective consciousness.

And like the boy in the film, despite the large numbers we did manage, it wasn't large enough in my perception. I felt like the boy in the *Paying It Forward* film, downhearted that I couldn't see the wide rippling effects.

However, since that moment in time, I have been aware of a deepening of a message that wants to come through about the importance of aligning ourselves with the Universe, so we can be true to who we are, honour who we are, know who we are and live in the world according to this principle.

As we do so all of the dark shadow side such as control, manipulation and fear diminishes – hence the tools in this book that are here to prompt activation in the next levels of your alignment, allowing yourself to see your wonderful essence for all its glory and create something aligned to your purpose. We will work on ways to increase your alignment and therefore create the true beautiful bounty in your life.

Stories sometimes demonstrate how it all works, stories I feel are one of the best teachers around, they stay in our mind and hearts with an archetypal power.

I have a wish that we all come together in beautiful alignment, for the sake of 1 = self, each other, the Earth, the sky and the sea – I was going to say the Universe – but the message I got was "You think the human race is responsible for the highest good of the Universe? Don't be so arrogant!" I feel what is meant by that is to let go of any martyrdom/guilt complexes we may be carrying when we think of what we have done to the world, all it does is attach to us, weigh us down and make us arrogant in believing we know what is right in the world. Instead, if we open ourselves up to listen, hear and embrace what is being whispered in the winds about how to act in the present moment, then change has a chance to happen.

How much scepticism, judgment and criticism have you found for yourself as you read this last chapter? Ask yourself not to be judgmental with your judgment, but just to bring it into a new level of consciousness and ask it why it's there?

Let's not take my word for it. Let's connect you to your feelings about what the Earth is going through…

You may want a pen and paper…

## Seeing the Earth's Soul

Close your eyes… take a few minutes to relax by focusing your attention on your breathing… imagine or intend that you melt down into the core of mother Earth, connecting with her heart… feel her pulsate through your being… now ask her the following questions… below.

The trick is not to judge what comes, but just allow free-flow, without concerning yourself as to whether the information is 'true' or not, at this present moment. You are practicing answering with your gut/heart/emotional centres rather than your head.

1. What was the spiritual reason or purpose of the First World War?

2. Why were there two World Wars so close together?

3. Is there a pain blockage in the Earth? If so where is it? Please show me or tell me what I need to know about it.

4. What was the spiritual reason or purpose of the Japanese Tsunami?

5. Why is the number 11 or symbol of II so significant in the World Wars, Tsunami and Twin Towers?

6. What is the purpose of the economic downturn?

7. What can I do in myself to help the alignment?

8. Please show me the energetic imprint of the world currently (you may see different colours around the globes, shapes, textures etc).

9. How does the world wish to be? Please show me energetically (as above).

### Seeing Your Soul

Consider for a moment who you would be when you take away all of your roles? Not mother, father, son, daughter, boyfriend, girlfriend, job title, friend. In every relationship a different part of us comes to the fore. Release them all now and tune into the depth of your very being. Your soul knows no limitation or pain, the very deepest aspect of you is always free in every sense of the word. Close your eyes and tune into it now, how does it feel or appear to you? You may find it magnificent to paint a picture of what has been shown to you as the essence of your soul, your truth, your calling, and any words to describe it too. This picture will only represent your soul right now – it is always evolving, but it is a powerful exercise in clearing your energy, connecting to and seeing who you really are right now.

As an example, when I did this I saw a gigantic golden orange ball, with red around the outside and I got the words warm, powerful, creative, bold and passionate. I then instantly felt a massive energetic shift. So I do this exercise even without the painting – just with my intent every time I feel depleted in some way.

### Seeding Your Youniversal Plan

Now you have seen your soul and the soul of the Earth you may want to let your soul's energies merge with the Earth's – just by seeing it happen in your own mind's eye and by doing your own little intention of working together for peace and harmony throughout the world. You may know what the plan is for you, or you may not. It is not important. All that is important is the intention to merge, which you have otherwise you wouldn't be reading this. By using intent and visualisation consciously we are sending huge ripples of Co Creative and Co Collective energy across the world. It's a strong message and activation for the path of your Youniverse.

Funnily enough whilst re-writing this chapter I began to see 11, 111 and 1111 everywhere... The number of people who like a post, or comment on Facebook. In my bills and printed on receipts. There were even 111 participants on my first webinar. I drove from Cornwall to London and the number of '11s' I saw on number plates was ridiculous! Yes I was looking for it, yes I was on the road for a very long time and yes I was on the M25 in rush hour. However, I was waiting for a car to pass me before I came out of a parking bay at Reading services, and the other car was waiting for me, we ended up playing a nudging forward game with each other – and their number plate? F11unny! The next day I woke up to 111 emails, 111 messages on Facebook, and I imported a list into my database, the notification of completion informed me that 111 addresses had been added!

## Chapter 4

# The Chariot

### Mixing and Mastering the Elements

*Only one who devotes himself to a cause with his whole strength and soul can be a true master. For this reason mastery demands all of a person.*
– Albert Einstein

So now we are at chapter four; let's take a deep breath in … and out … aahhhh … and now apply our intention. Let's re-cap, re-group and re-member what Co Creation is. I say remember because we all know. It's deep within every one of us.

I have assigned this step of the journey The Chariot due to its association with the astrological sign of Cancer; Cancer has a strong identity and attachment to the past. Cancer is a product of the past and through that it knows exactly where it has been and where it is heading. The Chariot has to keep the two polarities of self and Universe blended in perfect balance, which is the secret of Youniversal Co Creation. The Chariot must not tip too far in either direction on the roaring journey of growth so pertinent to each of us in today's fast-paced race. Risks of tipping include getting too strong a will, being too attached, too greedy, too inflexible, too proud and basically too egotistical. But the opposite can make The Chariot tip too, not enough will, too little attachment, too much flexibility, too much humbleness.

In other words to be a good Co Creator there is a need to strike the right balance. This feels like a journey we are all on, doesn't it?

Let's look at some warning signs that your Chariot maybe tipping too far in one direction or another.

## Signs of Too Much Ego

- The need to control.
- Feeling responsible.
- Feeling rushed.
- Feeling stressed.
- Feeling insecure.
- Feeling like you need to fight for what you believe in.
- Feeling like you aren't being understood or supported.
- Feeling fear.
- Feeling judgmental.
- Feeling self-pity.
- Feeling like you must possess.
- Feelings of greed.
- Inability to let go.
- Inability to wind down.
- Feeling guilty.

When we have too much ego it becomes impossible for the Universe to work with/through us. The self gets full of too much 'you' and not enough 'Universe'. Cutting off from our lives becomes harder and harder, an ever increasing struggle. It is a downward spiral. The more cut off you feel from the Universe, the more you believe, attach or cling to the needs of the above list, blocked by fear and will.

## Signs of Too Little Ego

- The feeling that all is meant to be like it is, so what's the point in trying?
- The feeling of resignation.
- Feeling demotivated.
- Feeling zombified.
- Feeling of couldn't care less.

- Feeling like you can't be bothered.
- Feeling like what's the point in trying to speak up or stand up.
- Feeling comfortable.
- Feeling a disinterest in worldly affairs.
- Feeling self-pity.
- Feeling like you just want an easy life.
- Inability to stand up for yourself.
- Inability to get your point across.
- Inability to get going.

The title of this – too little ego, is a little misleading, as it is still the ego at work here. This demonstrates that anything out of balance is egoism. On one hand we have the uptight ego, on the other the demotivated one, either way we are still full of too much self, 'you', for any Co Creative 'Youniverse' to happen.

I suggest that by going through the lists above regularly and marking yourself on a scale of 1–10 for how strong these feelings are in you at this present moment, may help you to see how in balance you are, or whether you are becoming too asleep or too driven. Just like on the motorway we have signs about not driving whilst tired, we also have speed restrictions. This is an important step in self-diagnosis around how Co Creative you are right now. If your score is high do not worry, once something is seen then you are only one step away from changing it.

### So What is the Perfect Blend for Your Youinverse to be Ignited?

- Recognition that our life possesses a wider identity than that in our limited awareness.

- An awareness that the thoughts and feelings that come

through us are not our own, therefore it is not our responsibility to get attached.

- An ability to determine which thoughts and feelings are useful, and which are clean or clear in their vibration, e.g. from the Universe and not other people. Basically, thoughts and feelings from the Universe feel light, instant, clear, easy, refreshing, inspiring, freeing. Thoughts and feelings from others feel heavy, murky and confusing.

- Understanding that as long as we stay aligned to the light, we will be looked after in a way that is real and doesn't pander to ego, illusion or fear. We will be supported in a way that makes life aligned and free.

- A commitment to staying aligned e.g. acting on our inspirations with a determination and a knowing faith, rather than an attachment. Recognizing that our inspirations are not ours. We are the aerial to pick up and broadcast out.

- An understanding that in order to keep sending out a crystal clear message across the world we must frequently tune back in again.

### If there is 'too little ego', work with...

- Recognition that we do have a purpose, we were born with one, and by not discovering it, we are not living to our fullest potential, we are dead whilst alive. By allowing ourselves to explore the things that interest us with fun and exploration in our hearts, we begin to rediscover who we are and from that our purposes begin to bloom.

- Awareness that while everything maybe how it is meant to

be, we are an integral and important part of that creation. That movement, that journey of progress and evolution turns everything into how it is meant to be.

- Open to inspiration by watching inspiring films and reading inspirational books.

- Create motivation to act on inspiration by giving ourselves permission to do things differently.

- Nurture our health to feel awake and alert.

- Allowing ourselves to feel passion and excitement at the thought of working with the Universe to bring about its will on the Earth. A good way to do this is to just take a nice deep breath in and as you breathe out imagine the energy in your crown releasing and opening up to the Universe, practice releasing and letting go. All you need to do is clear out and relax, it will come when you are receptive but not pushing.

- Recognizing the power of the words you speak (to yourself and others) and use it in a still, calm and resolute manner.

- Take time to track the journey of growth and make a list of all the ways you have grown or changed, or what you might have achieved in the last few months, year, ten years, or anytime in between. The list doesn't have to be full of big achievements, they could be small, humble achievements that only you know about – remember that all that matters is that these are significant to YOU!

- Practice feeling connected to the world at large, even and especially when all you are seeing is disconnection.

Practice looking through what you are seeing and feeling, the connection is there underneath, always.

- Practice feeling sensitivity to all in the world, a shared compassion and a bond. Find an easy way to do that; for instance, it may be easier to practise with animals at first: spend time with them, but don't escape in them. Practice feeling that same level of love with everyone you meet AND everyone close to you. I emphasise that last part because ironically it seems easier to give strangers unconditional love than people close to us sometimes.

- Practice feeling like you want to live your life purpose to its fullest potential and giving yourself permission to. I must emphasise the last part because without giving yourself permission you may end up feeling like you want to but can't, therefore reinforcing victim mentality. No one is going to give you permission, except you. Visualise a gauge going from 1–10 and see where the needle rises to when you ask yourself how much permission you are giving yourself. If it's not high don't resist it or try to change it, just note that its existence signifies that there is more to discover about why there is resistance. Relax your energy field to release resistance, rather than closing up and fighting it, which will just keep your resistance-to-resistance up!

Blending these attributes aids you to be riding on The Chariot of Co Creation successfully, primed for the Universe to work its magic with you in your Youniverse.

## Chapter 5

# The High Priestess

### Working with Imagination, Intention, Intuition, Integrity and the Id

*Your Imagination is a preview of your life's coming attractions.*
– Albert Einstein

The word 'psyche' has a double meaning, it means 'mind' as well as 'soul'. We are conditioned to think that it means mind only, just like we are conditioned to using the mind only. We are over-identified with the mind and under-identified with the imagination, or in more words of Einstein, "The intuitive mind is a sacred gift and the rational mind is a faithful servant. We have created a society that honours the servant and has forgotten the gift."

The intuitive mind is a mind that can access the sub-conscious and make it conscious, and the imagination is the bridge to make that possible. Therefore imagination is the key to turning on our Youinversal satellite. Without an imagination we are literally turned off. There is no passion for life. In fact there is no life, no inspiration, no hope for creation. Nothing came into being without first being imagined. Yet imagination gets some hard flack, its right to exist is constantly under attack and invalidated – 'It's just my imagination'.

Imagination is a right-brained function getting flack from a left brained world. In the left-brain we have reason and logic and in the right we have imagination, intuition and creativity. Remember The Chariot? The secret to successful Co Creation is getting the right balance, but we are conditioned to rely on our left brains and see the right brain as unreliable, making us scared to access it and the result is imbalance. But nothing is to be feared, only understood…

## The Story of the Five I's
## Imagination, Intention, Intuition, Integrity and the Id

*First, there was imagination, made from a beautiful ball of vivid colours. But imagination was so alone she didn't know what to do with herself. The magical colours she held were stunningly beautiful, but what was the point if nobody saw them? What a waste indeed. Slowly but surely loneliness, isolated imagination and purposelessness caught up not far behind. In a depressive state, imagination went for a walk. Looking at her imagined feet and not where she was going, imagination bumped into intention. Intention was so different to imagination. Where imagination had bright colour, intention was a cool range of greys. Where imagination was formless, intention had structure. Imagination and Intention realized that they were the missing half of the other; imagination and intention had found a soul mate in each other. Suddenly life was complete, full of purpose, they felt like there was nothing they couldn't achieve together. And they were right. But there was one missing ingredient…*

*The human.*

*So, one day, Imagination and Intention decided to go humaning (like fishing), as they began to reel/real in humans, they 'real-ized' everything including themselves and the humans was limitless. Imagination and intention merged with the humans and they realized by entering one, they had entered them all. Humans were astonishingly connected – but humans weren't able to see or experience that for themselves, not without Imagination and Intention. This was because humans already had something in them called the Id.*

*The Id itself was the landing place for imagination and intention, as well as the launch pad. The Id was the missing ingredient, but the Id came with two other sides to its being: the super-ego and the ego. These parts were also necessary, without the ego the Id would be a passionate bubbling cauldron of explosive chaos. The ego gave that powerful combustion of a cauldron some control, but along with the ego came the super-ego. The super-ego is an ultimate perfectionist that drives humans forward in their evolution, but it is critical in more than one way. The super-ego loves to criticize nothing more than the ego; in turn the ego gets highly defensive.*

*"Oh lord!" thought Imagination and Intention as they looked at each other. Intention said to Imagination, "That's another fine mess you've gotten me into!" And so began the complex journey of consciousness. Intention started so clear and fresh, but got so confused during the melding process. Imagination started so vivid and magical, but got pangs of ridicule as the super-ego reduced it back down to nothing, pushing its well-known buttons of purposelessness. But Intention and Imagination weren't to be beaten at the first hurdle, oh no. So they dug a little deeper down through to the core centre of the human where they found the most powerful place of all. The heart, and in the heart they met feeling. Feeling was pulsating with life – I guess you could call her pregnant; yes feeling was pregnant – indefinitely and always. Pregnant with an unknown possibility of new life, this new life was called Intuition. So it was here in the heart, that Intention and Imagination found the pure state needed for Co Creation.*

*Whereas Imagination had the hardest time with the adult human, it was far easier for Imagination to work with the egoless state of new life. But it was hard for intention to remain straight and upright within the new life, as the new life just wanted to play and Intention was just too serious. Intention started to feel out of place as it went through lots of childlike tantrums. One day poor old Intention was feeling particularly bruised and battered, he had been swung by his imaginary tail one too many times like a used and abused, yet beloved, play toy. Flung to the curb he tried so hard to rise up again, but his will was feeling so downtrodden he wasn't sure he had the strength. Then all of a sudden, Intention heard a creaking and rustling sound rise up from deep within the mound of worn-out play toys, that had piled up from mounds of discarded experience. Intention turned his head to see a tree rising up.*

*But not just any tree, oh no siree, this was the tree of integrity, which we will call "Integretree". Integretree was a huge, beautiful majestic oak, so robust. Suddenly matured from seemingly nothing so very quickly due to the vast amount of manure/experience. All the time Feeling was flinging Intention around, the perfect conditions were actually being created, the fields of growth.*

*Integretree reached out a loving branch and helped Intention to his feet. Integretree's deep gnarled eyes and old cracked mouth captivated Intention as if he was in a hypnotic state, and in that interlocking moment Integretree boomed to Intention "grow with me". The relief Intention felt was enormous as he merged and grew into Integretree.*

To this day Integretree grows within each one of us. Sometimes our Integretree is a deeply gnarled and twisted tree, a tree that forgets to reach for the light through states of pure confusion. Sometimes our Integretree is clear, because it remembers that its purpose is to grow high and tall and earthed and grounded, a perfect Co Creator.

"How do I know that it isn't my imagination?" is one of the most common questions in my work. The answer is "It is your imagination"! As well as your intuition that is, and you are working with your intention to access it. It is not imagination that needs work, it is integrity, and once we have integrity we can distinguish that which is gnarled and twisted, and that which is straight and clear. In short, intuition will grow and as integrity and intuition grow, so will the straightness in our core where we develop a deep trust or inner knowing.

Our imagination is the filter that projects information from the subconscious to the conscious, the rainbow bridge of the two worlds. Everything stems from our imagination. It is our most powerful gift. First there was imagination – nothing in our world came into existence without being imagined first. Imagination is stronger than the will. Don't think of the colour pink will you?

What just happened?

Our imagination is not our problem, it is our power. The problem is interpretation, working on our intention and integrity is the secret in getting it right. The phrase 'it's just my imagination' is probably the biggest invalidation of our biggest ever gift. Now, is that because society knows how powerful we individuals would be if we realized the power the imagination holds? We all know the statistic that we supposedly only use a third of our brains right?

Using our imagination and subconscious are right-brained activities, as is any form of art or creativity. But again, look at the beliefs in society, that if we pursue a right-brained career we will be wasting our time: the struggling artist, or the boy who wants to be a musician but his father says he has to become a lawyer; the daughter who wants to be an actress but her mother tells her she should work in an office. You get the picture?

Have you ever asked yourself why society is set up to crush individual expression? Time and time again I see people unhappy in their jobs but too afraid to leave and honour the calling of their own individuality. It is a scary thing to do yes, and we are trained to fear it through societal beliefs that the left-brained world is the only reliable one. There seems to be two common beliefs out there.

1. A job is not something to enjoy, God forbid! – It is something that pays the bills and for your hobby; and as for the 'hobby' you enjoy doing, well that wouldn't pay the bills and even if it did…

2. Doing your hobby as a job means you wouldn't enjoy it anymore!

Both of these beliefs are rooted in fear – it is expressed in different ways but it serves the same function – to block you. So lets tackle these one by one:

With the first belief, that you can live your life in alignment with your purpose and passion and pay the bills, it is important to believe that you can. Okay, maybe it doesn't mean you can quit your corporate career and run a ready-made successful business overnight, and it may mean you will need to look at what you are hung up on that is stopping your progress – like the big fat bonus for example, or the fear of maybe not being able to pay your bills. But, if you don't change something how is it ever going to change? Perhaps it is harder to do if you have got used to a certain standard of living, but if you have that comfort zone then you can use it to help you build up your true passion alongside, so at some point you can sidestep. Freeing up your imagination and beliefs to shift your perception of hobby verses career is the bridge to carry you across.

If you don't have the corporate career, then you don't have the luxury of choice to do that, but then again if you never had it you won't be accustomed to a certain standard of living and it may be much easier for you to make the transition. Again there is a call to free up the imagination and your beliefs in order to shift your perception of hobby verses career to access the bridge to carry you across.

So as you can see, both cases look like they have opposite challenges but it actually fundamentally comes down to one common shared challenge. The challenge to imagine, dream and create it into being.

Personally, I feel blessed in never having a great education or the corporate career. Brought up by a struggling artist single parent in the country, meant that I started my adult life by leaving school at fifteen, scraping GCSEs in Art, Drama and English only, then going into low-paid jobs in retail or care. When I moved to London in my early twenties I was already burnt out. Sitting in meditation with a ring in my hand belonging to my father figure who had passed away a couple of years beforehand (who was a warlock and incredibly good at astral travel. In fact, looking back, I feel I was having more communication with him at that time than when he was alive – but I quite often felt it was my imagination!) I asked in my head what to do about my career and I heard clear as day, "Open a healing centre or shop, it has to be in Camberwell." This was shocking for me – I had never dared to imagine that I could achieve such a thing. However the message was so strong that when my then boyfriend came home I said to him, "Do you fancy opening a shop?"

"Yeah okay, in a few years perhaps."

"No, now. Do you fancy doing it now?"

Shocked, his response was, "Yeah, right okay, I will take you more seriously when I see it happening."

Six months later I had a business plan full to the brim with field and desk research, forecasts, cash flow projections, suppliers, costings etc … but still no money. We were living like students. Nevertheless we went to the bank who were so gobsmacked by the size of the business plan sitting on their desk compared to the scribbling they usually got on the back of an envelope, that they sat us down and took two young student looking hippies seriously. However, the computer said "no" when we applied for a limited company, or other set ups. But I had become aware of a brand new set up – "limited liability (ll) partnership", and we asked the bank to run with that – bingo!

So now we had the plan and the pounds, but not the property. We found one almost straight away but we weren't sure about the location and everyone was telling us location was everything. However, after much deliberation we realized it felt right to us so we put in an offer – the day they withdrew it from the market!

Gutted and desperate I found myself printing letters out and walking around Camberwell (which translates as 'crippleswell' and yes it is a pretty poorly part of inner South London) putting the letters through any derelict or empty shop/building I could find. One letter left and my conscious head and intent knew exactly where it was going with it. But suddenly I heard in my head "Stop – put it in here." I turned round and saw where I was, outside the shop we originally fell in love with. In went the letter and I went home to pack for our holiday. As I opened the front door there was a letter laying on the mat, it said, "We are selling the flat you are living in do you want to buy or move out?" As I was reading it the phone rang, it was the owners of the shop interested in our offer. We spent our holiday deliberating – mortgage or shop (and secretly I was also wondering mortgage, shop – or university?).

The shop won and a year later we were open. A gorgeous shop that dripped like Aladdin's cave, with a secret chill out basement and a backroom for therapies and readings. We just happened to be right next door to the methadone clinic and two minutes away from one of London's largest psychiatric hospitals. People used to come in and exclaim, "A crystal shop? In Camberwell? The only crystals people are interested in here is Meths!" I'm not saying it was easy, but there was never a dull day!

Like any new business we were in debt for the first two years and began making money in the third, when we decided to close. People thought we were just as mad as when we opened. "You work your butt off for three years, just start making money and then decide to close?"

But I knew I couldn't grow anymore. Isn't that interesting? That as soon as our bank balance started growing the growth of my soul stopped. I am not saying you can't have both – I believe you can if you listen to the thoughts and feelings coming through you about how to change with it. Perhaps it's a magical road of twists and turns that gives us the real riches of life. I shut shop. Most people would have seen that as a waste of three years or a failure, but all I saw was a massive achievement. I knew that never again could I go back into employment. I had found who I was and that to me was priceless. And because I knew who I was, things literally came to me, not necessarily in the way I expected or at the time I wanted, but still they came because I was clear about who I was and what I wanted in my life. I don't think I would be where I am in my career today without that experience; or if I had kept the shop, chosen university or a mortgage.

I knew exactly where wanted to work. I walked into Mysteries in Covent Garden and asked for a test reading. I passed and then I rang every week for six weeks to try to get a start date from them, to no avail. On the sixth week I put the phone down for what felt to me like the final time. "That's it, I'm not ringing them again," I thought.

'"Yes you are, you are ringing them on Friday," boomed a crystal clear voice in my head, one that shocked the living daylights out of me. Awareness of my clairaudience had kicked in three years earlier, yes, but I was still getting used to it and had a belief that it was something subtle (which it is most of the time). Never before had I heard something so individual, so defined, so loud and so against my own thoughts. It was so obviously not my voice in my head, and so began the argumentative relationship I have with my guides!

"No I am not!"

"Yes you are."

"No I am not!"

All the time that this was going on I was thinking about how crazy it/I was!

Anyway, they didn't respond to my second objection, they never do! They allow me to learn for myself and learn for myself I do, usually in an excruciatingly painful way!

That Friday morning I opened an email from my ex saying, "Hey I met a guy in Thailand, and we were talking about being in contact with exes, and he is in contact with his ex, her name is Tiffany and she works at Mysteries but she's leaving soon."

My God! Okay, I get it, it's Friday and I am ringing! I pick up the phone and say for the seventh week running, "Hi, it's Tiffany."

"Oh hi, Tiffany, yes, Tiffany is leaving, would you like her place?!"

So why the delay? Well who knows! But I ended up with a ready-made client base taking over from someone with the same name! People didn't even realize! So often they would say, "Oh yes you told me that six months ago," and I would say, "Erm no, I haven't been here that long – that must have been the Tiffany before me."

"Oh yes! I thought you looked different!"

"Look different? The other Tiffany was tall thin and blonde, oh yes! I underwent plastic surgery to become short, dumpy and brunette!"

As you may see from my stories, in the ways that I am the listening or trusting type, I am in just as many ways the arrogant, untrusting and controlling type too. I am a Leo with a Taurus ascendant – translated that means bloody one-tracked and incredibly stubborn. The time I spoke of earlier, about being in meditation, in those days was few and far between. After years of practice I have reached fifteen minutes or half an hour a day. The easier meditation practice for me is a movement one called five rhythms, which to any onlooker looks like it involves throwing yourself around like a loon for two hours. And still I am not conscious enough to get it, oh so painfully, often! It takes some pretty strong messages and synchronicities to happen. I'm so glad that I have such persistent guides. I often wonder why they bother, but as my husband says, they need someone that bloody persistent to make it happen, and they know once I do get it, that's it!

I shared this story with you because that was the time my life forked so clearly – was I going to go mainstream, or…? And at that time my clairaudience was the strongest it had ever been. I was practically being told what to do. If I look at it as a singular experience it would be easy to say the shop failed, I failed, and my guides set me up for a fall. But I don't see it that way. I saw the shop as the University of Life teaching me how to be self-employed in the spiritual arts, and I loved that feeling of being in line with who I was. I was excited to start reading at Mysteries, ever since I had set foot in there years before, I knew that I wanted to read there and this road led me there, and getting work there led to ... well, let's go there after we address this part...

The second belief is that if we do end up doing our passion as a career, then yes, perhaps we won't enjoy it so much after a while. But we will be SELF-employed, and therefore no one can limit or expand what we do, except ourselves. By not honouring our gift/purpose/passion/identity (whatever you want to call it), we may well be invalidating our core gift of growth, for ourselves and the world, effectively causing inner and outer misalignment and blocks. By allowing our hobbies to become more than just a hobby we have growth and creativity oozes if allowed to, passion will continue to create and grow and there will be no room for boredom.

Saying, "If I do my hobby for a living I will get bored," is like saying that if a tree grows it will die of boredom. Not allowing growth ultimately causes boredom and death of feeling alive. The truth is if you are self-employed doing what you love, then you are the one and the only one who holds the power to grow with it or not. It's ultimately you. We are told that self-employment holds no security, but it holds no limits either. Does today's world hold any security anyway? In fact was security ever a reality? Or is it all just an illusion? Is anything actually guaranteed apart from death? But death is only life on the other side – so another illusion. The scary thing is that living the dream doesn't come with a step-by-step structure. We have to create the steps. But if we remember that we are part of the Universe and allow ourselves to be guided, to listen to our feelings and follow our gut instinct, we realize that we do have a step-by-step structure after all, it's just one that's felt and not necessarily seen.

So, from being a shop owner and psychic reader, I became a psychic reader and teacher; from being a psychic reader and teacher I became an author. From being a reader, teacher and author I started TV presenting … and I am really excited to see what happens next! This is growth, but it's growth of a different kind. It's not growth where you are pushing against yourself because you are repressing what you really want to do and working your guts out to get the next promotion (unaligned growth that causes dis-ease). It's a natural, flowing, blossoming growth from the soul, spirit and purpose, so how then do would we ever get bored with doing our 'hobby'?

The imagination is either a block or a key, depending on what we do with it and how we interpret it. Repressing it doesn't do much good either; it will build up like a volcano. Just like The Tower card in the Tarot, which happens to be dealt to the person who dreams of a different life, but takes no steps to build it. They are the person that is likely to find the different life eventually happening to them – but not necessarily in the way they want. Use your imagination wisely before it uses you, it's your most powerful gift.

So let's go back to the very beginning point, about how imagination is not our problem, it is our judgment that's the problem. So often it is easy to either devalue imagination, or overinflate it. I still devalue it now. Only the other day, whilst watching a film, I said to my husband that I felt cold. He asked me if I wanted him to relight the fire that had long since burnt out. I said no because it was so close to bedtime. He went upstairs and I carried on watching the film, after a couple of minutes I became aware out of the corner of my eye that the fire was burning, my first thought was "Oh My God!" But then I calmed myself down with a logical explanation – he must have lit it before he went upstairs. When my husband returned he looked at the fire, looked at me and said, "You witch," and sat down as if it was normal! It was me that had a problem accepting it and I'm the one that stresses to others how important it is to trust their imagination!

I de-valued my imagination with my estranged father too. When I was twenty-eight I spontaneously saw a past life, where he was employed by me as a cook. I saw him peeling off the top layers of his skin with a knife and putting it in my food and I knew this was something he did on a regular basis. But for the next seven years I believed I had imagined the whole thing, because I had not been aware of any synchronicity happening to back it up. Until one day seven years later when my mother calls to tell me of my father's obituary in the local news – he died of Scleroderma, which translates as 'hard skin', a very rare degenerative condition where hard skin grows very slowly around all your internal organs, slowly strangling them. I went for tests and I was clear, now if that's not karma in action what is? That very day I had woken up from a dream where I was dying of a skin disease caused by being eaten by fleas and leaving it too long to be treated. Other realizations started dropping into place for me very rapidly for the next few months. I had always seen my father as the planet Saturn, and it clicked that Saturn rules the teeth, skin and bones, and that in mythology he ate his children. Saturn is conjunct with my Sun (at the time of my birth Saturn was in the same place in the sky as the Sun was); I have literally been 'sat on' by Saturn/Satan all my life. My Sun is found right deep down at the bottom of my birth-chart so my light is well hidden (even though it is in Leo) and Saturn being so heavy has kept me down, but throughout the years I have got stronger and stronger – like using Saturn as weights for training.

My first book launched on the 7th September 2012 and my dad died on the 8th, which felt like a something shifting with Saturn. But still I thought I had imagined it all at first – and I had, but not in the way that we are taught to think of imagination. The way that says it's not real. Really imagination does conjure up stuff, but stuff from somewhere.

There is a subtle difference between really working with imagination and visualizing on purpose. The danger with visualizing on purpose is that we may be disconnecting ourselves from the Universe. There are beneficial ways to work with visualization, but if we become attached to it then manipulation can easily find its way in, which heralds the lack of trust and before we know it we have then become the archetype of the dark magician, spoken about previously.

Working positively with imagination and intention is more about becoming awake to the thoughts in our head. It's all about opening 1 = self to ask questions. Below are some pointers about how to work with your imagination for alignment. You may find it helpful to start a journal for your daily practices.

## Daily Practices to Increase Your Co Creative Imagination, Intention, Intuition and Integrity

Below are ten practices to integrate into daily living to boost up your connection to the Universe. If it feels overwhelming to practice all of them straight away I suggest picking one from below – no need for a numerical order to it. Whatever one jumps out at you will be right for you right now, practice it until it becomes second nature and then move on to the next and so on. Better that each one is mastered properly than all half attempted.

1. Keep in your mind the idea that you are an empty vessel, always connected to the Universe and ready to receive from it at any time, as well as being ready to ask about anything at any time. Release the need for the answer – particularly a need for an instant answer. Be awake and open rather than attached. This sets the powerful message to the Universe that you are ready to work in

aligned Co Creation, opening to your Youniverse. You may get answers coming back, and if you do that's great, but the practice is in the opening and the asking.

2. Upon waking from any dreams send your thoughts up and ask what is wanting to come through from that – don't expect to get an answer right away, or at all. It's all in the practice. It can be handy to start a dream journal, try to do so for at least a month, then review how you feel about continuing or not.

3. As you get dressed notice what clothes you feel drawn to wear. Is it a practical reason? One of social conforming? If so, is there something you can wear underneath to help you feel connected to your own individuality? What colours are you drawn to today? Has your style changed lately? In what way? What change does this signify in you? Is there a change of your spirit guides? Again send thoughts up about why that might be, notice how you are feeling, these questions are here for you to start your dialoguing with the Universe, but the answers don't usually come back as they do in normal communication, they can do sometimes, but usually when you least expect it!

4. What thoughts are going on for you about the day? Are they fearful or excited? Depressive or light? If they are negative get to the root of it; there's going to be fear in there somewhere that you are not going to get what you need and if left to your imagination it can run wild on that unconscious trip, which is the opposite of what we wish to achieve. So if you do feel negative remember you do have your own hotline to the Universe, and remember that all is not as bad as it seems. How many times do we

stress ourselves out over a situation that is not as bad in reality as it is in our heads? Or maybe we stress ourselves out about a situation that has happened. Stop! If it has happened, it's happened. Be kind to yourself and choose good thoughts. And also know that this paragraph may need to be read time and time again. I have just done this very thing the last few months, kept a lot of stuff in. When I finally allowed it out I realized it was much worse in my head than it was in reality.

5. Take time to breathe deep, relax and open your heart by allowing yourself to feel the love that is always in there somewhere. Even if you find it hard to do in your current state, the hardest step is to begin; once you have begun you will start to feel better. It is important to connect with the Universe in a relaxed, loving state. I am not one to believe that we have to sit down and dedicate ourselves to a meditation practice to do this; if you want to then that's fantastic. But I feel the danger is in thinking we have to dedicate time to access that state – so we never really do. I feel it is necessary to remember that the most important thing to do is to wake up to what is running through our head and hearts, and recognize anything that feels heavy. Once we have witnessed that, we can then say, "Ah okay, I am open to this changing." It is that very act of intention that is the catalyst, just like in Quantum Physics, as soon as an atom is seen it changes. Meditation increases our awareness and therefore our ability to do this, so if you struggle with natural awareness arising from intention then a meditation practice can help. In fact I have started meditating regularly and do believe meditation has massive benefits for everyone, but not everyone sits and does it, so I am giving you ways to meditate on the move so to speak.

6. Once you have become awake to your thoughts and feelings you can start to talk to the Universe about what you feel you need, though not in a demanding, fearful or mistrusting way. When does talking in that manner to anyone result in success? The Universe is no exception. Practice talking in a way where you clearly and responsibly explain what you feel you need with the energy of confidence and calmness. This is imagination and intention working together at their best. But also remember that you are a micro and the Universe is a macro. Leave room for remembering it knows far more than us and include that in any communication. State that you are open to receive what you feel you need – or what the Universe feels you need for your highest good and growth. Quite often when I had a day of working with clients at Mysteries I'd tune into my thoughts. I'd notice the clients that were in my thoughts were the ones who would show up that day. I would also ask for how many I was likely to see, and if I was not happy with that number (either because it felt too many for me that day or not enough), I would ask why it was that way, and then if I still felt it needed changing I would ask what I need to know to change it for the highest good of all. I would then start to feel a Co Creative blend happening with my day. The same went for working on the phone lines, which is a challenging line of work for a reader and I noticed it would go far better if I did the above steps than if I didn't.

7. Throughout your day listen to your thoughts and feelings during your activities, if anything feels heavy ask yourself if there is a different way to do this. It's about slowing down enough to have the realizations. Even if you feel you can't change the situation you are in, you can change your attitude to it. Wake up to your feelings, they are an

inner compass, if something feels heavy then choose what feels the best for you in that moment.

8. Throughout the day be open and be non-expectant, but ready to take notice of any flashes that happen, albeit visually, auditory or kinaesthetically. And in particular also be aware of your reaction to it. Is there any fear there?

9. Become aware of your self-talk when fear happens, what is it serving? Do you resist it or play yourself down? Do you criticize it or yourself? Is judgment arising in you? Do you attach? If so practice noticing it, acknowledging it, letting it ride through and saying thank you. It's okay if something you receive isn't in line with what you want; we were given the gift of free will. Just make sure you are releasing it because you really don't want to do it, rather than fear masquerading as you really don't want to do it! Remember you can communicate with the Universe at all times, you can send a message in your thoughts asking why you have been shown this, and what you need to know about it.

10. Most of all, open your heart, open your mind, see each day as a sacred creation, and remember your part in it!

# Chapter 6

# Death

## Developing Truth, Trust and Transformation

*Personal transformation can and does have global effects. As we go, so goes the world, for the world is us. The revolution that will save the world is ultimately a personal one.*
– Marianne Williamson

We all know that Death is one of the most feared cards in the Tarot. Some of us are so scared that if we pull it we will die – if that was true I would have died hundreds of times already! But then again maybe I have done just that. You will be able to tell from the title of my books that transformation is something I am big on, and as I look back on my life there has been so much death/transformation. Death of my homes, friendships, jobs, marital statuses, names and the literal death of friends and family, all of which ultimately lead to a death of identity leading to transformation. It seems that we don't just fear death itself but death in any form of change, endings and transformations. There can be so much fear that even the quote "Just when the caterpillar thought the world was over he became a butterfly" brings little comfort when we are building up to the change.

Death in the Tarot is a long drawn out process, as can be transformation. It's not always seen as such though, it depends how tuned in we are in the run up. More often than not we just like to ignore it, block it, stick our head in the sand and sing 'la la la' in the hope it will stop us from going gaga. Yet Death (change/transformation) is the very thing that stops us going gaga. You just have to look at how we hold off death for as long as possible nowadays and the problems this can cause. Holding change at bay is an expensive business, one where we pay with our lives one way or another.

Yet Death (change/transformation) is your greatest ally, the one who appears because your life is now outgrown and is blocking your growth. Just like the seasons, there has to be winter for new life to be born and growth to continue. Yes, it is one of the most painful transitions to go through as we cannot help but grieve for that which has died in our lives; and sometimes we can't even see why it had to happen, it's very painful not being able to understand why. I guess that is the hardest thing about life, the lack of understanding about why things happen. Hence the hunger for understanding as some antidote for suffering, and I do believe that understanding is an antidote to suffering hence my dedication to it. Below is an archetypal story about the process of transformation, which I believe we are being asked to do in these current times in quite a fundamental manner.

## Understanding the Triple Ts , Truth, Trust and Transformation

Carrying on with the exploration of the human where we found imagination, intuition, intention, the id and integretree – well there were more trees. Trees, of Truth, Trust and Transformation. Truth was so magnificent, the tallest of all the trees. Trust was small and humble, modest and refined. Transformation was expansive, round and wide. They stood so close together that their roots and branches merged; some days they grew together so beautifully that you could almost hear the blissful harmony they were making. On other days they bumped and clanked against each other, crying out for the space and freedom to express who they were. But the thing was, they really were one. The separation was actually an illusion, their lesson. To realize how to live in beautiful Co Creative existence of growth with each other, in fact, their very survival depended on it. They were family.

Truth was impregnated by Trust and in Truth, grew Transformation. But as Transformation grew he had the hardest time. He was a perfect blend of his parents, not too tall, not too short and beautifully expansive, but where he once saw his parents as essential to his survival, they were now clipping his branches and the wings within them. He yearned for the space to expand. As he grew into a teenager he became hedonistic in his growth and caused his parents much pain and disturbance. But his parents knew that they were his parents and stood still, not budging an inch of their boundaries. Even so, it was a challenging time for them all and it tested Trust and Truth to their limits, causing them to bump and grind against each other. This time not in beautiful Co Creation, but in a screeching inharmonious manner, and sometimes they too wished they were separate. So you see, their purpose, their lessons, their growth was all entwined, all interdependent. And although Truth and Trust were great role models, Transformation had to go on his own journey, he rebelled by reaching out to other trees. Trees that weren't so unique or original in their essence, trees that were clones, factory trees devoid of any expression, devoid of Truth, Trust and Transformation, trees that he wanted to be like. Transformation yearned to free of who he was. He saw Transformation as hard work and he just wanted to have an easy life. Plain and simple was the way he saw the other trees and he saw much beauty in that. The more beauty Transformation saw in the others, the fewer acceptances he felt in himself. And so he began to grow, off-kilter.

Transformation managed to find the gaps to grow around and reach out through as he began to merge with the other trees. At first the other trees only mirrored back to him his own issues with self-acceptance. He wasn't one of them, he didn't look like them and he came from a different place. He was an outsider. But Transformation learned fast and he knew how he had to grow to impress, to transform himself into not just one of them, but the most impressive one of them.

At first Transformation loved all the adoration he was getting, it helped him grow tall and proud, but as he got tall and proud the other trees started to feel intimidated. They did not possess any truth or trust so they carried on admiring Transformation to his trunk, and behind it they would whisperingly moan and bitch about him, those gossipy whispering trees. But even though Transformation had rebelled from his parents of Truth and Trust he was still very much part of them; he could recognize easily anything that was untrue and the ears of his leaves reached far beyond the visible perimeters.

Transformation felt the illusion of the beauty he had once seen shatter and he broke from his core, the weight of his misaligned growth became too much to bear. Transformation came crashing down angrily, tearing down the clones along with him. The clones were no more, but Transformation began to grow again, from his true core.

Transformation was welcomed home and there he found acceptance – of himself, his parents, his nature and his part to play. To this day Trust, Truth and Transformation continue to grow together gracefully, spreading their beautiful harmony out into the world. Transformation is now so vast and expansive his seeds drop wide and far, his purpose is huge in the Universe and now he knows he is nothing without Trust and Truth. He knows the importance of connection and how being closely entwined does not cut you off from where you should be. Being where you are and closely entwined gives you the support to grow in alignment with where you are. Feeling natural, easy and graceful.

How are your three trees doing?

### Your Three Trees of Truth, Trust and Transformation

See yourself as the Transformation tree, and as you ask yourself the following questions; give yourself full permission to jot down absolutely anything and everything! This is more like a cleansing exercise; don't worry about what you are writing, just go for it!

1. Are you in resistance of your roots/heritage/home/family in any way at all? Jot them down, if you can't think of any at first rack your brains – there will be something!

2. Why are you in resistance of it?

3. How is that playing out in your life?

4. Are you growing off track? You will know the answer to this because it lies in any situation where you feel out of balance, harmony or truth. Jot below any areas in your life that feel that way.

5. What changes could you implement that may bring about a graceful change of growth?

6. What are you realizing from all you have written above?

The story of the three trees is mirrored throughout the beginning stages of this book. Firstly in the story of Lauren, about how her pairs of chromosomes split 'incorrectly' to cause a third, resulting in a syndrome. But then, miraculously, they split 'incorrectly' again, resulting in 'correction'. However, the chromosomes that split incorrectly beforehand stayed, so in a way the result was damage limitation rather than 'correction', maybe just to make sure she did have some time here to do what she needed to do. The three trees are also represented in the story of The Fifth Element, the two world wars and the synchronicities I had resulting in the 'Paying It Forward' world meditation.

One of my favourite guides is Marcus Aurelius, the meditation below is taken from his Meditations book and says it all…

> *A branch cut off from the adjacent branch must be cut off from the whole tree also. So too a man when he is separated from another man has fallen off from the whole social community. Now as to a branch, another cuts it off, but a man by his own act separates himself from his neighbour when he hates him and turns away from him, and he does not know that he has at the same time cut himself off from the whole social system. Yet he has this privilege certainly from Zeus who framed society, for it is in our power to grow again to that which is near to us, and again to become a part, which helps to make up the whole. However, if it often happens, this kind of separation, it makes it difficult for that which detaches itself to be brought to unity and to be restored to its former condition. Finally, the branch, which from the first grew together with the tree, and has continued to have one life with it, is not like that which after being cut off is then grafted, for this is something like what the gardeners mean when they say that it grows with the rest of the tree, but that it has not the same mind with it.*

Trees are silent symbolic teachers of how to live, grow and Co Create. The growth of a tree is dependent on light (consciousness) the tree has to turn this way or that way to grow towards the light, or it may just stay stunted. By walking through a forest we can see why trees grew the way they did and this can be a powerful walking meditation on understanding our own and others' paths of growth. I am lucky enough to live on the edge of a forest and anytime I have a hard time accepting others for the way they are, I go for a walk there. It helps me to remember that everyone's path of growth is unique and different due to the factors weathered and it helps me to understand or at least accept that their path is the way it is for a very good reason. It's the closest I can get to walking in somebody else's shoes and coming out of any judgment or emotionality around an issue. If I can understand why a tree has grown the way it has, then I can understand why a person has grown the way they have, even if my mind can't see it clearly, this practice reminds me somehow. I strongly believe that all pain arises from misunderstanding, so any practice that aids understanding brings great relief.

So what are the keys here?

Acceptance? Grace? Harmony?

Well I guess grace and harmony grow from acceptance and from acceptance springs all things to do with love and spirituality? It's a tricky one isn't it? Knowing when to be accepting and when not. Like the serenity prayer by Reinhold Niebuhr – *God grant me the serenity to accept the things I cannot change. The courage to change the things I can, and the wisdom to know the difference!*

Let's look at the power of acceptance and how it works in Truth, Trust and Transformation:

1. If we are accepting, we choose to accept the truth. From that we gain the ability to see clearly and from that we gain humility and grace. This does not mean we are accepting anything we are presented with as gospel, it means accepting that certain things are the way they are for a reason. It doesn't mean buying into a charade because we are accepting it, it means staying awake to it. It means we give ourselves permission to see things as they are, at least for us, and it doesn't mean swallowing everything.

2. If we are accepting, then we are trusting; not necessarily of the person or the situation, the trust goes higher than

that. We trust that all is as it should be rather than trusting that the Universe will give us that which we are attached to. Which actually isn't trust at all. So many times we say, "I put my trust in that person/situation and they let me down." But we actually didn't. What we really did was give our power to that person or situation. Putting our trust/power in something or someone is a lower, stilted, small way of being. Putting our trust in the Universe is something much higher, vaster and infinite of course, but still the word 'trust' can actually imply so many forms of dependency, manipulation, attachment and control. So really what I am talking about here is developing a 'knowing' that all is being divinely guided. The danger when I say the previous sentence is that it can sound as if I am advocating shirking any responsibility for our lives onto the Universe, but this book is all about getting the balance right. For Co Creation to take place and our Youniverse to happen we have to be larger, freer and expansive enough to receive and implement.

3. If we are accepting, then we are transforming because we are not in resistance of whatever is changing in our lives. We may have a habit of thinking that acceptance keeps us stuck. That we need to fight to get what we want and sometimes that is true. However, looking back through my life at the times I have grown, healed and transformed, the most it has been when I have been in a place of acceptance. Firstly, acceptance gave me the ability to face the truth. Secondly, acceptance gave me the trust that I could take on board what it was showing me. Resulting in the transformation, which came in a beautiful feeling of natural goodness of growth and improvement.

## The Four Virtues of Acceptance
## Truth, Trust, Transformation and Love

Ask yourself the following and just jot down ANYTHING that comes to mind – give yourself permission to be uncensored!

1. How are you with accepting the truth? I know it's not always easy to know what is true, so maybe I should say how are you with accepting that which life presents you with?

2. How were you doing with trusting the Universe (and not manipulating it through attachment to agenda) before you read this book? Be honest!

3. How are you doing with it now?

4. Are you seeing any signs of transformation in your thoughts, words, emotions, actions and manifestations? What are they?

5. Are you seeing and feeling any changes in the way you love yourself? If so what are they?

6. Are you seeing and feeling any changes in the way you love others? What are they?

7. Are you seeing any synchronicity occurring in your life, if so what new life is it pointing towards?

# Chapter 7

# The Wheel of Fortune

## Fulfilling Graceful Opportunities

*Faith is a living, daring confidence in God's grace, so sure and certain that a man could stake his life on it a thousand times.*
– Martin Luther King

Yesterday I was holding a workshop on Co Creation. In it we did the measure of grace exercise found earlier in this book. When the participants were asked if they had faith that all was working for their highest good the answer was almost a unanimous "When it's going good, yes!"

That made me laugh! It's so true that it is easy to have faith that life has your back when all is going well isn't it? But is that having faith? When things are going good there is little need for faith, its existence becomes almost dormant. The practice of faith only really kicks in when things are challenging.

Faith and grace are interrelated. If one has faith then one has grace. Grace is a humbleness that recognizes so called blocks in one's life as relevant, even if we don't understand why. Actually faith and grace come fully into play especially when we don't understand why. Faith and grace are a gift of love to ourselves. With faith and grace we can bow down, take a step back and look at how to flow around the so-called obstacles instead of banging our heads against them.

Below are a few stories about my own journey with recognizing grace.

## The Art of Grace

**December 2012 – Dance studios, Sevillia Spain.**

"Natalie, I can't move like that, I'm not that trained, or flexible!"

"Tiffany, show me YOUR dance."

Natalie put on my music and I lost myself, moving in the zone, in the flow rolling all around the floor and climbing walls!

"That's why I love free dance, Natalie, something comes through... But ask me to do steps, and well, I am not graceful enough."

"Tiffany, grace is a word I associate with you whenever I think of you."

"Really?"

"Yes, you are full of grace, the way you have coped with the things life has thrown at you, and, in particular, I always feel astounded at the amount of grace you have shown around losing Lauren."

I was shocked! My judgments told me I am too unrefined in my physicality and personality, too edgy, too raw, too quirky/weird/odd, too arrogant/stubborn/strong-minded, to be graceful. I was astounded by what I had just been told. It was one of those rare precious gifts, a perception given back from the outside world. This observation had the power to crack me open, to give me light where I thought there wasn't any. Almost as if I was a seed of grace that stayed a seed, because it didn't think it had any grace so it didn't bother to grow. But along came my friend and sprinkled words of grace as she spoke and as they landed on the seed of grace it felt happy, full of life, and finally it found a passion to grow.

Since that day I have been thinking long, hard and deep about the concept of grace. I have come to the conclusion that I am more graceful than I thought and there is always more room to become more graceful.

The other day I had to walk through Oxford Street to get to my live TV shift. I was late and as I rose from the underground I was faced with a sea of people all jostling each other in a chaotic ocean of different directions and currents. I stood for a second, wondering the best way to approach this and 'Girls Just Wanna Have Fun' came on my iPod so I guess you could say I bellyflopped into the crowd – well not quite! But the way I merged into it had the same qualities of knowingness, trust, fun, connectedness and love. I concentrated on any little space I could see and flowed into it, even if it took me off my supposed path and had me spinning. My own judgments of where I needed to go would have resulted in me being beaten up by the different currents if I had stuck to them. With an intention set of where I needed to go but the ability to give way, the grace to bend, flex and dance around the others who had just as much right to be there as I did, I actually arrived a lot quicker and a lot happier.

My friend's comment about something she saw in me that I never saw, has served a life-changing purpose in me. I have never told her what an impact that had on me and I won't now as I love the thought of her reading this and seeing for herself. That is why it's so powerful to be open and share – you may not see or know just how life changing what you share is, but a simple sentence has enough power to create a whole new outlook, words = 'spelling', and spelling creates magic.

## The Story of Rada

One gloriously hot day in the summer of 2013, I found a secret garden tucked away in central London. Sitting there on my lunch break a man walked along and said "WOW!" as he looked around at his surroundings – he had such a gorgeous smile of light which he looked at me with. He asked if he could sit next to me. I trusted his smile, so nodded and he sat down. He told me he hadn't been here for a long time and it had got very wild. I said I had only just found it and I had worked round the corner for seven years. He started saying that life is funny like that, how we go round and round in circles for seven years and that we make all these grand plans of travel and other things, but really it's all there right in front of our nose and that's the very reason we don't see it, it's too close.

I actually do go through seven-year cycles, I am a number seven and I was going through a seven-year cycle at the time and it was exactly what I needed to hear. I asked him if he had seen Joan of Arcadia, he hadn't so I explained that it's about a girl who meets God every day in the form of someone out in public and how I felt that was just what happened. He said that it was all about how you look at things in life and that my sunglasses were made of God consciousness! I really had to go but didn't want to seem rude, so asked him if he was on Facebook – he wasn't but asked if he could email so I gave him my card and told him my name was Tiffany. He said he was Mark, but to people he feels a connection with he is 'Rada' and to call him Rada. I looked up Rada as soon as I got back to work – it means joyfulness (and in Czech it means advice!). He said it was nice to connect with someone so open and free from judgment or fear. I guess that is the only way we can receive joyfulness or advice.

The above story is full of grace and magic because we were both open enough to go with the unexpected flow and happenings in the present moment and our words created magic. Magic I will never forget, even though I didn't see him again, in fact, especially as I didn't see him again.

### The Graceful Swan

As I came back to edit this chapter I happened to be reading a book called *The Dance of The Wounded Souls*. In it the author Robert Burney speaks about the book contained in *The Medicine Cards* by Jamie Sams and Dan Carson. It is the story of Swan medicine. The story talks about how Swan came upon a huge swirling dark vortex and a Dragonfly. The dragonfly is one of the most ancient animals still in existence, showing us the power it holds through the past and magical transformation. Dragonfly explained to Swan that the vortex was the doorway to imagination, how he had been the guardian of the vortex for many, many moons and how if she wanted to enter she would have to promise that she would not resist whatever happened to her, instead she would need to fully embrace and accept all as part of the Great Spirit's plan. Swan was hesitant at first but then stated that she had decided she would honour and not fight whatever she went through in the black vortex.

"So be it!" said Dragonfly as he hovered to the edge and Swan got sucked in to the swirling vortex.

When Swan re-emerged a few days later, Dragonfly was taken back at her long-necked elegance and radiance purity. "Swan, what happened?" he asked.

"Dragonfly, I learnt to surrender my body to the currents of the Great Spirit within the vortex and developed huge faith and acceptance, which meant I was granted the ability to see many great futures because I have achieved a state of grace."

Yes! This is it! In so many ways…

Firstly, the story addresses the dark night of the soul. In our culture we tend to skirt around it resisting the pull of the vortex because we fear where the dark night of the soul may take us. We constantly stay in a resistant state, blocked from imagination, blocked from developing grace, blocked from transformation. But if we can make a vow to ourselves that we do not resist the Great Spirit's plan then we really have nothing to fear and everything to gain.

Secondly, I really do believe that the vision of the future only belongs to those who can remain unattached and in non-resistance. I believe that in my practice I can tell which clients are most likely to be able to create their future or not, because I can see quite clearly whether they are resisting the vortex or not. The story of Swan represents the truest deepest initiation of grace and I hope it comes to your mind next time life throws you something you wish to resist, but in the meantime…

## Graceful Opportunity 1

Why not take the chance whenever you can to offer something graceful? My friend's comment about my gracefulness was full of grace itself. It was authentic and offered generously from the heart, with no agenda. The meeting with Rada was a graceful offering that we allowed to happen. Moments and words like these have the power to change people's lives for the better. So whenever you really feel your heart overflow with goodness and gracefulness why not share it? You could start today, you could start right now. You could get up right now and go tell someone something you feel in your heart. Something you may have never shared with them, but could well change their perception of themselves and their life. If they aren't around then why not call them, message them, or even write them a letter. Remember to do this with a pure heart, something true that you are letting out of your heart, like a butterfly of love… Feel the beauty in setting it free, knowing that you cannot know its journey and it may never return, but that's the beauty. It actually feels right to set it free, the moment of liberation feels so full of beauty and freedom that it's a sacred ritual there in itself.

## Graceful Opportunity 2

Remember how good it felt to do the above exercise? Make a commitment to yourself to look for 'graceful opportunities' every day. Practice being open from your heart and setting free any graceful flutters, then truly feel it. Just make the decision to open up and share it. Notice what happens, you may find that more synchronicity comes into your life and people just come to life, or that some aren't too sure how to take it. It is a sign of change in either case. Even if they don't seem instantly open to it, my bet is they are feeling positively affected on the inside – it may even be a moment that they may remember for the rest of their lives.

## Graceful Opportunity 3

I am sure you can think of a moment when one of those graceful butterflies was let out of someone else's heart towards you, and as it fluttered around your own heart how your life changed? I bet you are deeply grateful but you never told that person just what a deep effect it had on you? So then, if that is the case, can you imagine the ripple effect of 'graceful opportunities'? You may never know the far-reaching effects, but that doesn't make it insignificant. It makes it beautiful. It makes it a humble deed not done for recognition but just for the sake of it. Perhaps though, you may feel now as if you want to open your heart to that person, and allow a little love butterfly of recognition or validation of what that meant for you, to fly towards them.

One of my students did this very thing the other day. She was feeling disheartened with the psychic phone line work, a classic issue. She spoke about how someone wanted a prediction and she told him or her that it didn't work that way, and even if she wanted to she wouldn't be able to. The person told her she was a bad reader and hung up. It was something that used to happen to me a lot too so I suggested that she didn't focus on the obstacle, but the way forward, concentrate on where she could go and help the client to rephrase the question.

This evening I received this lovely graceful butterfly:

> *Today I have had a profound experience, I feel. I wanted to share the experience of one of my readings with you. Without wishing to disclose or discuss exactly the content of the reading, it is more about the outcome. In that the spread for this person was about seeing the reality/truth, which in turn led the person to reveal the number of readings she had invested thousands of pounds in over*

*the last four years, keeping them stuck in a place of disempowerment, until now! I am now finding Tarot reading to be the most rewarding way of working, and I am so grateful for your way of teaching, so wanted to say thank you Tiffany for the difference you are making and to appreciate the huge effort you put in to what you do.*

What a lovely graceful butterfly she set free, to take the time to let someone know that his or her presence made a difference can make all the difference.

By opening up to share what is in our hearts we are really starting to Co Create, as long as it's authentically there to share then you are putting Co Creation into action. Through the process of sharing, the Universe will be seeing that its flow is not wasted on you, for you are prepared to honour, share and give birth to what is coming through – your Youniverse.

The next story of grace was written whilst on a yoga juice detox retreat in Turkey.

### Grace is in the Air

Yesterday a wasp landed on me whilst sunbathing at the poolside. I tried to be really Zen about the whole thing as it was crawling all over my bare skin, telling myself it was an opportunity to connect with the wasp through meditation, after all, it wasn't looking as if it was going to sting me! As soon as I thought the words 'going to sting me' that was it, I was up leaping around (our subconscious doesn't hear negatives) and the wasp fell off me into a puddle of water by the side of my sun-lounger. It fell in on its back and was desperately trying to get on its front, wings soaked, legs flapping in the air, sting going ten to the dozen. I felt so guilty that I attempted to help the wasp (who was a needless victim of my fear) by trying to flip it over with my book – repeatedly! But all I managed to do was attract the attention of the other retreaters who said, "Tiffany! What are you doing?"

This was day one of the retreat and on some level I think they had already clocked that bizarre behaviour was something to expect from me – especially when I walked right through the middle of the group at the arrival lounge in the airport expecting to see another group behind, and then turning round with a rather red face when there wasn't one. So I explained what had happened and that I had just read this great book called *Am I Being Kind?* And even though I am not supposed to, I now suffered from guilt – something I never really suffered from before, and it was okay I would recover, but I didn't think the wasp would, in fact I thought I was torturing it! So I opened my bottle of water, screwed up my face and poured it over the wasp whilst chanting "Hare Krishna" (to allay my guilt you see – except the guilt that most of these retreaters were first timers to any of this kind of stuff, and I might have been scarring them for life that is). I then looked at the wasp – yep it looked pretty still. But much to my surprise a couple of minutes later it got up! Looking very damp and not at all impressed it limped under my neighbour's sun-lounger to recover – and recover it did. Ten minutes later it was up flying around and I felt so much better – until it landed on my neighbour who turned to me and said, "If it takes its revenge on me, I will kill you!"

Not surprisingly after writing about letting graceful butterflies out of the heart before bed that night, I dreamt I had a pet wasp in a plastic cage but I couldn't keep it, and I had to open the plastic cage and set it free. It was a bit scary as it emerged but I felt much better afterwards. Talking about this at juice and psyllium clayfast this morning, one of them said,

> *"Aha! So you see when you let out butterflies from your heart, you let out wasps too – you let go of the things that sting you."*

I thought that was rather profound for silly o-clock in the morning, and I made a mental note that it was going in the book

– but I can't take the credit, I only typed it.

That afternoon in the pool a beautiful flying colourful dart kept diving back and forth, fluttering to and from, dancing around and skimming the surface of the pool. We couldn't work out if it was a butterfly or a dragonfly, and as I said, "Are you a butterfly or a dragonfly?" it flew right at me! Hovered and fluttered in one spot in front of my face as if to say, "What do you think?" And when I didn't get that either, it did it again! I still didn't get it and so it flew past the retreater who happened to be a Geography teacher who was just arriving at the poolside. "That's a swallowtail butterfly," he offered up, oblivious to the fact that he had just answered a burning question for my new pool friend and me who had just bonded over the butterfly – oh and the wasp. I felt as if the butterfly was saying to itself, "Thank god for that!" The weirdest thing though, was that two weeks ago I saw a dragonfly flying around a tree, it was so big I was confused. I had only ever seen small dragonflies around water, so I thought, "No, it must be a bird," and as I thought that it did what this butterfly did. It flew right in front of me and hovered there as if to say, "I am no bird!"

In fact the amount of connection I am having with flying animals at the moment is profound and not just flying animals, but flying mammals! Yesterday I replied to a Facebook message from a client, asking for a session. She responded that she had just arrived back from a yoga retreat 40 minutes away from Fethiye. So I replied that Fethiye was near where I was and how did she know? She told me I had my location switched on – doh! But it turned out that I was at the hotel next to where she was and we had crossed in the air! She also said that she had spent all week thinking, "I must contact Tiffany," and it had taken her until the day she left and I had arrived to do it! Graceful connection is in the air it seems, huge synchronistic signs staring me in the face since I have been writing this chapter. So let's look at this 'Grace is in the air' statement.

## Graceful Opportunity 4

In the Tarot thoughts are associated with air; ask yourself how graceful are your thoughts? Score yourself from 1–10 about your thoughts and how you spend your time with them, 1 being not a lot of time, 10 being all the time:

Hurried
Stressed
Anxious
Judging
Peaceful
Accepting
Loving
Serving happily

Compare the positive with the negative. Perhaps you can even see what triggers any ungraceful thoughts, and maybe you could look at what to do about that. Is it a change of life internally or externally that is called for?

In the Tarot, air is associated with communication. How much time do you spend with yourself or with others doing the following (score yourself from 1–10. 1 being not a lot of time, 10 being all the time):

Arguing
Criticizing
Demeaning
Blaming
Soothing
Encouraging
Supporting
Sharing

Now compare the two. Perhaps you can even see whom or what triggers any ungraceful communication and maybe you could look at what to do about that. Is it a change of life internally or externally that is called for?

In the Tarot, air is about travel, how much time do you spend moving in a way that is the following? (Score yourself from 1–10 1 being not a lot of time, 10 being all the time.)

Stressed
Hurried
Battling
Selfishly
Flowing
Patiently
Enjoyably
Respectfully
Expressively

Now compare. Perhaps you can even see what triggers any ungraceful movement, and maybe you could look at what to do about that. Is it a change of life internally or externally that is called for?

It is interesting that this evening just before I wrote the above I was receiving a talk about the eight steps of Raja yoga. As I listened I thought, "Yes! That's grace!" Now don't get me wrong, I am far from a yogi – which come to think of it, is one of the reasons I think I am ungraceful. Whilst others sit peacefully in the lotus position, chanting "Ommmm my body is a temple," I have been known in the past to sit with my knees around my ears and my back rounded, desperately trying to stay upright muttering, "Ummmm my body is a shit house." I guess I have got better, my knees are still pretty high, my back still a bit rounded, and I still feel like the worst yogi in any class setting – but I definitely never tell my body it is a shit house anymore!

To be honest, I have always found yoga classes, and sometimes yoga teachers, challenging. I would much rather dance. There is one exception to the rule though, and that is my friend Lauren. Lauren and I have a very special connection. It began the day my then boss announced there was a new girl called Lauren starting on March 17th, which happened to be the day of my daughter Lauren's passing. I had never met anyone called Lauren before or after my daughter and knowing the power of names, I couldn't face the possibility of meeting a Lauren on the day of my daughter's passing in case I didn't like her, so I took the day off. On the 18th March I arrived at work knowing that I would have to face it, but I would have to sooner or later, and at least it wasn't on the anniversary of my daughter's passing. I walked in and the first thing I saw was Lauren in front of me. She looked at me and her face broke out in this beautifully warm, genuine smile. It broke all fear I had there in the moment because it was like love at first sight! I felt it was not the first time I had met this soul, (which she also confirmed she felt later) and without words we embraced! That was twelve years ago now and she really is a beautiful source of peace in my life, one that nurtures my soul with a spirituality and love full of purity.

I found out Lauren's main passion was yoga, and if any yogi that I know of walks their talk in a humble and graceful fashion it is Lauren Manning. Tonight she had treated us to a talk on the eight steps of Raja yoga. I heard her (once again) speak with love, clarity, compassion, conviction and passion, but this was the first time I heard her (or anyone) speak so deeply of the philosophy of yoga. It was wonderful and it had the dance of grace written all over it.

The Asanas (physical postures) are only one limb of yoga, when the philosophy behind it is embodied we get the true results in the grace of the physical Asanas, they are merely an outer reflection.

## The Yamas – From the Eight Limbs of Raja Yoga (Eight Steps to Enlightenment ) – Sage Patanjali Maharishi

The Yamas are five moral codes found in the first step to enlightenment within Raja Yoga. Practicing authentic integration of the Yamas through thought, word and deed, brings about a strong foundation for grace/enlightenment and therefore Co-Creation. They are as follows:

**Ahimsa = Nonviolence:** In mind, word and deed. A famous case of the power of Ahimsa would be Gandhi, the way he changed the world so powerfully by taking a nonviolent stand. To me the biggest form of violence in the mind is judgment, whether it is good or bad, on another or 1 = self. It keeps us dangling within an inch of a fall from grace and in a way it is a form of arrogance (and as I type this – I start to wonder if I am being arrogant for judging judgment!). It's such a natural thing for the mind to do. I don't think we can stop judging, it's an instinctive part of human nature. But if we start with the practice of waking up to when we are judging, realizing we are doing it and choosing not to then surely we are on our way to non-violence? I will finish this with the words of Gandhi who said, "Thoughts change the world, so make sure your thoughts are good ones, good thoughts become good words, good words become good deeds."

**Satya = Truthfulness**: Now, truthfulness again starts with the self, how can we be truthful with others if we are not truthful with ourselves? But then there are sayings about the truth, on one hand that it hurts and on the other that it will set you free. Can you see the interchangeable balance here? The Yamas say it is also important to be non-violent in mind, word and deed. As I listened to the eight steps tonight I realized the one I had to develop the most was the non-violence. I don't believe I am a violent person in my actions, but I believe my thoughts and words can be and that is because I am a truthful person. You just have to look at the title of my series *The Transformational Truth*, I believe passionately that the truth does set you free, that it empowers you like nothing else if you can get past the fear and face it. But I have been learning a lot over the years about how forcing it on people is not respectful, humble or correct. I try so very hard now to moderate the strong calling I have to speak the truth, without lying and without hurting and as a result my life is becoming far more peaceful, unified and graceful. This is the interchange that is spoken of here.

My grandfather is one of the most spiritual people I know and he always used to say to me, "Tiffany, if you can't say anything positive, don't say anything at all!" So I have never been one to gossip about others or be two-faced, but when it came to telling the truth – well that is where I fell down. I just couldn't be a party to anyone's delusions, but now I am learning how to do this with a respect for their situation. Blurting out the truth (as I see it) is only helpful if done at the right time and in the right way, with the right words and the right energy. This doesn't mean I am compromising myself if my intention is always one of authenticity and transparency – which it is. It just means I focus on me, myself, and if someone asks me for my take on the truth of his or her situation I will give it. But delivery is key between healing and hurting, which is an intricate balancing act.

**Asteya – Non-stealing:** Apart from the obvious this also means not stealing another's ideas and making them your own. Can you imagine what a wonderful world it would be if everyone knew that no one else was going to steal anything, even his or her words or ideas? How open people would be? It would be amazing! The power of openness heals. I have made it part of my practice to be open and I see the most closed people melt around that, transforming their lives. But still there are times I close, due to fear or just plain laziness and without openness we miss so much. An example is of the story I told you earlier, about my client being on the retreat next door. I probably would not have known that if Facebook didn't tell her where I was. We miss so much magic in life, huge undercurrents of the stuff when we don't feel safe enough to share. I am lucky that most of the time I feel safe enough to share, but even so there are times I have felt that I shouldn't share. However, it is mirrored back to me pretty instantly that I should abide by synchronistic happening, which shows me how I nearly missed so much by not being open. Keep that in mind next time you feel that perhaps you shouldn't share. Sharing has an incredible domino effect; it gives other people permission to relax and open up, to feel strong in their vulnerability too, which is true strength. Yes it's vulnerable, people may judge us or steal our ideas, but it is also incredibly powerful and we stand to gain far more than we may lose. I realize I have spoken more about the truthfulness Yama in a sense here. I have concentrated more on not being afraid that people are going to steal from you, rather than the non-stealing aspect. Which is interesting. Perhaps I feel that the non-stealing is pretty self-explanatory, and that if none of us worried about the perception of stealing, then perhaps stealing wouldn't exist? I feel the same about this as I do about people feeling used. I have never got that perception either. We are all humans with a purpose to serve, right? Saying you feel used is to object to your very purpose, isn't it? And if you feel really used then it was you that let yourself be used, right? Personally I never feel used, I guess sometimes it must happen but I never feel it or worry about it. I feel a need to emphasize the domino effect – positive or negative that comes from non-stealing or stealing. Someone who has been stolen from is far more likely to walk through life closed and so much is missed. It would be great if everyone read this Yama and made an unspoken unbreakable rule about not stealing, but that is not going to happen … or is it? So I guess I want to emphasize the need to go through life not living in fear of being stolen from. Very hard for these days of insurance, suing, illegal downloads etc… I guess the way to see it is tied in with the other Yamas, which show a trust that all is as it should be, no matter what. The other day I had to share something with someone and it would have been so very tempting to say, "Don't tell anyone," but I could feel my energy shrink each time I thought about saying that line and decided not to say it. It may mean there are repercussions from sharing it but if there are, there are. Personally I feel freer for having shared, and in a way that I didn't put any stipulation on it.

**Brahmacharya = control of all senses:** I think in today's world we all yearn for this. The overstimulation we are bombarded with by the media. We can do things like stop watching TV and reading newspapers. In fact only in today's yoga practice Lauren asked if someone wanted to pick a number for a meditation from one of Louise Hay's books and what came up was Louise saying, "Let's write to the news and tell them we want at least 75 percent positive news, until then we will boycott it." The funniest thing was the lady who picked the number had a dream the night before that she was being inundated with newspapers she didn't want! It can be so hard to extract 1 = self in today's modern living. I remember when I was ten, I moaned at an adult because they had put the news on and their reply was "When you are older you will realize how important it is, you won't be able to live without watching the news." I made a decision right there and then that I would never watch the news and this I told them, and I never have. Some people think this is ignorant and I can understand that. One old friend comes to mind. She would watch the news, get totally distraught and just live every day completely and utterly upset. I tried to explain to her that her doing this wasn't helping anyone, let alone herself. She just thought that I was ignorant, arrogant and cold and I felt that spending her life feeling more and more powerless every day really wasn't helping anyone, but somehow she equated pain with caring. And I guess we all do this to some degree. The need to be in pain to show we care. Again it's about waking up to that. I guess we all really know that to change the world we have to start with our own world. Yet the challenge to stay focused on that is immense. Our feelings guide us with this though; the minute we get pulled out of ourselves we feel it. You know it – it's not a nice feeling – it's a feeling of unrest, anxiety and overwhelm. It can be addictive to bombard our senses with information, materialism, substances or other pleasures, but it never makes us feel good. When Lauren spoke about this she also used Oxford Street as an example and she spoke about the many temptations. She said at first you may need to retreat from the outside world in order to not be tempted but eventually it would be about being able to walk down Oxford Street without getting tempted. I started to feel smug thinking, "Whenever I walk down Oxford Street I concentrate on the space and dance into it! Oh yeah!" But then I realized if Oxford Street was loaded with chocolate shops would I still be able to do it? Hmm! Pre-retreat, probably not! Post-retreat, feeling hopeful! It seems like Oxford Street is the Mecca for spiritual development – yes Oxford Street is a perfect example of how Lucifer works for the light!

**Aparigraha – Non-Coveting:** The yearning to have something other than what you have – this one may be last but definitely not least and is the most obvious one to do with grace from what I can see. This is something I see so much of in my work and of course I have been guilty of for nearly all my life too. How else did I get into Tarot? But I have learnt to work with the Tarot as a way of tuning into the rhythms of life and honouring them, rather than trying to gain control of something we will never have. Life is not here to be controlled and any attempt to control the uncontrollable only results in endless torture and obsession. More and more I see the incredible importance of this final Yama. In fact it is what this whole book is based on. The need to Co Create, to be aligned to the divine will rather than our own. So many times in my work as a reader I see people who only want to know what is ahead. I yearn (ha! Have to work on that!) to find a way for them to see that what's ahead all boils down to how they deal with the 'present' in the present. Yearning for something other than what you have is the deepest ingratitude, arrogance and blasphemy we all have the capacity to display. I couldn't see that I was graceful. I get hung up on things, I mourn and hanker. I know that there is a reason for things but if I don't understand them I end up in pain, hence my life has been so dedicated to finding understanding. But grace doesn't need understanding, grace is a respect, respect is giving something space to exist even if we don't agree with it.

My musings over grace have been transforming my consciousness in the most powerful ways over the last few months, like a springboard of realizations that have been waiting to see the light of day/consciousness for thirty-six years. In the past few months I have been aware of increasing feelings of intuition, synchronicity, happiness, connection, sacredness, humbleness, peace, trust, knowingness, love, compassion and respect in all aspects of life and with all living things. In fairness the intuition and synchronicity have always been there, but not alongside the other qualities! More often than not they came alongside trauma and drama, and I guess I was attached to trauma and drama because I felt the magic of synchronicity was linked to the creative element of drama. But grace is transforming that for me, showing me that synchronicity is present in everything. I feel my vibration getting clearer and higher as I am finding more freedom from attachment, and as this graceful practice is happening my vibration is rising to incredible levels. Only the other day I had such a powerful experience I feel it has left me with the same consciousness as someone who has had a near death experience.

I was doing a reading with a regular client, and we'd had a challenging session three months earlier because she was told some hard truths in a very strict manner. I thought perhaps after that she might not book again. But book again she did and we looked at everything but that subject – until the end when she just had to ask! As soon as she asked I felt an incredible energy come over me and into me, I started sitting differently, found my hands in a mudra (not something I would do) and speaking in a thick Indian accent. I was even rolling my Rs, which is something I can't do in my 'normal state'. I remember all that was said (which was the same as what I was saying, but with an energy of much more compassion and patience, much less ego and with more weight, more strength). Spirit had taken me completely out of the picture after last time and decided to speak to her directly. I remember sitting there dumbfounded speaking to them in my thoughts. "Wow! This is awesome! Please can you do this more? It's so much easier and better, just don't do it to me when I am on live TV, because it would get me into trouble!"

I have always had a strong level of faith, but this was something else. I came out of that experience really understanding, feeling and knowing that the only problem we have are our judgments. The ones that tell us we are separate, alone, isolated, abandoned, unsafe. I have really felt since that day that we really do not have anything to worry about, instead of trying to convince myself that we don't have anything to worry about it – and there is a difference.

I thought about why the reading had gone that way, and I put it down to love. I had been thinking about this particular client strongly since the last reading and I had been feeling for her. Not in a guilty way or a sympathetic way; I just simply felt my heart open for her and was aware the energy had been building over the month.

Yes, love is strongly related to grace. A true love is naturally graceful. To be graceful is a humble state of being, one where we realize that everything is right, as it is in the moment within its own divine order. It has just as much of a right to exist as we do, grace doesn't get angry at the blockages and obstacles. In fact it listens to them, honours them, respects them, glides around them, does them justice even. This is how we work with our karma and transform it into blessings.

My husband once joked with me that there was more empathy and compassion in a sweaty sock than in me, and he was right. Notice the past tense – yes, even he is seeing/saying it's a thing of the past and God forbid I think I might just be developing compassion! My judgments about others were strong, the worst one being that people should get over themselves, get out of self-pity and stop draining others. The victim mentality not only pushed my buttons, it had them jammed! A form of that in particular for me was benefit fraud. I felt that because of people who committed it, we were tarred with the same brush when I needed to claim benefits for Lauren. Because Lauren's condition was so rare they thought we were trying it on. The support came through, but only after she passed and I suddenly became livid for years at any benefit frauds.

There is a lot of seeming injustice in the world. But experience has taught me all is well. It's our judgments that bring pain and if something is in existence or happening then just because we don't understand it or agree with it doesn't mean it isn't serving a purpose, otherwise why would it be here? Just like flies. No one likes flies right? (Well I am sure there is someone out there who does, but let's just use the judgment that nobody likes flies.) Why don't we like them? Well because they are annoying little pests that have much fear of disease attached to them. They are too fast to catch and make an annoying buzzy sound that drives you insane. They don't look cute and you can't stroke them. They land on excrement and then your food, they throw up on your food and lay eggs on it and some bite you too! Yep, that's enough reason to not like flies. But their purpose is to clear up the mess in the world, which is a huge service to all other life on the planet. Maggots feed on decomposing bodies, helping to stop the spread of disease. Gardeners love hoverfly maggots because they feed on aphids. Fishermen love maggots because fish feed on them, and up the chain we go. Digging even deeper to purposes less visible is that they help pollinate plants. So now our poor bees are in trouble we need our flies even more.

If something is in existence then it has a right to be, for some reason, somewhere along the line, even if we struggle to see that. We are all on a path and even if we think that others are doing wrong, there really is a reason for everything. If it enrages us too, we end up involved in it, if we end up involved in it then we must have something to learn from it. I had to learn that getting angry with so-called victims was actually the victim in me. I was screaming out, "How dare you be so down! I've had it hard too you know; in fact I think I have had it a lot worse than you and do you see me complaining?" I have had a lot of counselling over the years and one counsellor said that what I was doing was not allowing others to have their pain, because I wasn't allowing my own. That I needed to start embracing and acknowledging my own pain. Wow! Another one of those life-changing statements/moments, the problem isn't pain, it's the fear/interpretation/judgment of it.

We really are looked after and guided and the only challenge we have is the lack of belief in that. And too right that it sounds conceited, ignorant or woo woo wishy washy when you look at the amount of suffering in the world. I can hear you say, "Try telling that to the mother helpless to do anything other than watch her child die, the homeless person, the prisoner of war, the abused child, the person who took their own life, or their friends and family left behind, or the person in the family of someone who committed murder." The list goes on, and in one way or another I have been a facet of all the examples above (less the prisoner of war – in the very literal sense anyway). I don't know what it's like to live a life of security and comfort – (that's a generalization – to a person in poverty, I live the life of Riley) and I think that could be because part of me feels that I would stop growing if I did. However I have learnt over the years that I really am in a Co Creative partnership with the Universe, I have seen the support in it time and time again. In turn I am learning I don't have to have a hard life to grow. I have learnt to trust that life may not always give me what I want, but it will always give me what I need. Now I am taking it to the next level, learning to love whatever it does give me and especially if it's not what I want! If I don't get what I want, then I know there's a bloody good reason why and that I must come out of my judgments and honour whatever present is in my present. And it is through my sharing that I hope you feel it too.

As I write this my mind turns to a beautiful present I just received from a client – did I want it? No! It was a gorgeous warm lovely homemade loaf of soda bread and he had made it with so much love! Why wouldn't you want that? Well because really it was a visit from angel irony! I had just managed to make myself practically carb free and I was supposed to be prepping for my yoga juice detox. So all day I was trapped in my room at work with the scent of freshly baked bread filling my nostrils, taunting me, not letting me forget the seductive little loaf of self-indulgent love. And yes I resorted to more than the smell filling my mouth. At first I told myself just a little nibble and delicately tore the tiniest piece, just to break beneath the crust into the warm, moist sponginess. Within 30 minutes those tiny pieces had multiplied like gremlins and I had devoured half the loaf! Call me psychic but I knew that would be the case when he presented me with it. So my first thought was "Bloody funny Universe – not!" But my baker client had said to me, "I was reading your blog and I saw that you had moved and bread is the best housewarming present traditionally. I also saw someone gave you something from Harrods and the tea towel this is wrapped in is from Harrods."

Click! The blog he was talking about was my most recent, all about how I woke up on Lammas (which translates as 'loaf mass' the festival of abundance) feeling naturally abundant with love, grace and gratitude. Not because it was Lammas or because of trying to work with gratitude to get more abundance, I was just feeling it. The day then unfolded in a magical way, I found myself the benefiter of other people's abundance. Gifted holidays and money appearing in my account, just as gifts of appreciation. With that I decided I could afford the afternoon off and went for a walk in the forest, where I came upon a pond full of loafs! 'Loaf mass!'

So I say to my client, "Oh yes you were reading the blog all about loaf mass and presents from Harrods. Did you realize you had decided to make me a loaf?"

"Oh my gosh! No I didn't realize!"

So even though I did not want the bread because it makes me feel heavy, I knew I wouldn't be able to resist it. I loved the gorgeous thought and act he had done. What he had done was to naturally Co Create with the Universe to remind me that I am receiving abundance through good-hearted people. He had literally done the opening poem of this book for me – a recipe for a graceful life. It was great timing too, maybe not on the physical plane, but on the spiritual plane it was perfect of course. Since Lammas I had been on a spiritual high. And the night before I came down with a thud. One too many practical demands meant I had crashed back down to Earth in a depressive manner and I was finding it hard to feel the faith or grace after a fortnight long intense ongoing connection to it.

Now, if I had gone with my first or honest feeling I would have said, "Thank you, that is lovely, but I don't eat bread as it's bad for me." I think you can see how wrong that option feels. I would have been showing ingratitude to him and the Universe. Seeing this in the way of the loaf-mass message, means I could have been sending out the message to the Universe, "Thank you, but I can't receive, it's bad for me, I don't trust that I will be okay with abundance, and I need to control my intake!"

It's all down to our judgments again. When I read this chapter to my husband he said there was an episode of Joan of Arcadia about grace. I mentioned the program earlier when I spoke about Rada. Joan of Arcadia is a young persons' program about a teenage girl called Joan who meets God in every episode through an ordinary person on the street; it could be the postman, the street cleaner, any ordinary Jo Blogs.

My husband brought Joan of Arcadia into my life, and his daughter brought it into his. All those years of Teletubbies he sat through whilst bringing up his daughter on his own were worth it just for Joan of Arcadia!

So I just looked it up on YouTube. It starts with Joan upset and blaming 'the ordinary man' for her winning a debate and losing her friend in the process. The ordinary man says she did wonderfully, she had found her voice, which was excellent. She yells at him about losing her friend and he responds by saying, "Do you know what grace is, Joan?"

"Yeah, pissed off."

"Grace is a gift of seeing life in an honest way, a new way, that can only be received when you are open enough," he replies.

I'm not saying we should lie back and accept whatever's thrown at us, or allow the resistance or judgment of a situation. Since when does fighting fire with fire, work? Sounds like a good description of war right? Is there any grace in war? An eye for an eye and the whole world goes blind, as Gandhi would say, and believe me, I have seen people fight so hard against the very thing they despise that they actually become the very thing they despise.

The trick is to find the space and move into it. If we all looked at the other cars on the road instead of the road we'd end up in a car crash. I've nearly done this too. I got so caught up in trying to read a logo on a lorry on the motorway I nearly ended up in the back of it. It was a big wakeup call on how important it is to concentrate on the space and not be distracted by the obstacle, and not just on the road. Concentrate on the space in life and move. Flow into wherever the space opens, release any agenda of where you are going and enjoy the journey. By making a practice out of finding the flow and the space we begin to see that the 'obstacles' are actually guiding us somewhere…

## Graceful Opportunity 5

A great practice is to find a busy street at least once a week (with or without your iPod) and practice gliding into the space. As you start to enjoy the process, up the challenge, something like needing to actually get somewhere by a certain time and see if you can still keep in with the enjoyment and grace…

## Graceful Opportunity 6

Think twice when you find yourself in a situation where you may not be open to receiving, or sharing. Whether it's something good like a present or even something like an obstacle.

## Head versus Heart

Judgments block us; take us out of the heart and into the head. In the heart we have grace, love, connection, spirituality, trust and creativity.

In the head we have criticism, fear, conditions, labels, pressure, it's like living with a *head master*… Let's look at some of those now:

## Graceful Opportunity 7

**Head**

The world is an unsafe place.
The world is an unfair place.
I must do whatever I can to protect myself.
It's not safe to be me.
I have to be untrue to myself to survive.
I am not good enough.
I can't trust anyone.

**Heart**

I know all is well and I am guided.
I am at peace with my world.
I feel love and connectedness with all living things.
I feel happiness in my daily activities and connections.
I trust the perfection of the plan.
I celebrate my own and everyone else's amazingness.
I know whatever happens with anyone is a sacred journey to honour.

Go through the above list and see how you react to each of those statements as you read them for each area of your life. For instance, you may want to start with career, then go on to relationships and so forth… See if they change with different areas of your life, what is this exercise illuminating for you?

# Chapter 8

# The Sun

## Working with the Ether for What Matters' Sake

*Rise up this mornin',*
*Smiled with the risin' sun,*
*Three little birds*
*Pitch by my doorstep*
*Singin' sweet songs*
*Of melodies pure and true,*
*Sayin', ("This is my message to you-ou-ou:")*
*Singin': "Don't worry 'bout a thing,*
*'Cause every little thing gonna be all right."*
– Bob Marley

In this book so far we have looked at why it is so important to be in alignment with the Universe and possible ways that may help your alignment. If you have been working on yourself with the exercises for at least 21 days you might just be feeling a difference in your vibration, one of less control, more freedom, joy and faith. One of being able to face 1 = self and work with the tough stuff knowing it's the magic stuff too. I say 21 days because that period of time is linked to making marked shifts. The 21 days to form a new habit is such a well-known belief that there is a myth that it has scientific back up, but yes that is just a myth. However, do we need scientific back up to believe anything or everything? I sincerely hope not! Personally I believe that if something feels helpful then go with it, what does it matter if it's true or not?

- In Reiki the cleansing period is 21 days.

- In the Tarot The World is the 22nd Card but numbered 21. The World card is the end of a chapter being the 22nd card. 21/22 is a celebration for working through what you needed to, successfully. The Tarot has 22 cards in the Major Arcana because the first card is actually numbered zero – so in a way The World is the 22nd card even though it's numbered 21.

- In the Kabbalah there are 22 pathways – one for each of the Major Arcana Tarot cards. The 22nd pathway is the last pathway to enlightenment joining Geburah (might and strength) to Tiperath (the heart and beauty). The Tarot card that joins might and strength to heart and beauty is Justice – number 11. In this book we have been looking at how 11 represents alignment to ourselves and the Universe, 11 also happens to be a master number.

- The Hebrew alphabet has 22 letters and Kabbalah teaches that the world was made out of these letters, The number 22 in numerology is another number standing for mastery – the next level up from 11.

Although the above facts aren't scientific, age old wisdom seems to imply that there is some kind of threshold we cross over at the number 21, one where we move into a manifested new life; we even see that in the coming of age on our 21st birthday.

Habits are long, strong ingrained patterns of behaviour that get woven deeply into our being, the more we do them the more programmed into us they get. The subconscious doesn't hear negatives so anytime we tell ourselves to stop doing something the resistance just gets stronger. When I worked with children who had autism we weren't allowed to say anything negative, we had to look for the directive instruction. "Stop fiddling" became "Put your hands on the table." We never used the word 'no' as it is a non-directive dead end. We found a way to nurture the life instead. This was powerful pre-training for my career (not that I knew it at the time). Even today at times where maybe I have said something nondirective on the phone lines click the phone goes dead.

I am talking about this in the chapter about working with matter (the brain) for what matters (the Earth) sake because now we have read through to a certain stage in the book and it's important to see how much your matter is mattering. I have assigned this chapter The Sun because the Sun represents our very being becoming conscious and knowing its own power. When the Sun is out it lights everything up, brings everything to life and we can see clearly where we are going. Our vision is crystal, indicating heightened consciousness and awareness. This is what we will explore in this chapter.

Firstly let's get back to basics. What things do we need to have in our vision before we start cooking? We need to see clearly in order to gather the necessary tools and information; this means that the very first ingredient to make anything happen is awareness. So for our working with 'what matters for what matters sake' recipe we need a big dollop of the following:

Awareness of our own judgments.
Awareness of limited conditionings … parental and societal.
Awareness of our own destructive patterns.
Awareness of our own limited belief systems.
Awareness of old paradigms of reality.
Awareness of lower self or egotistical agendas.
Awareness of stress and rushing.
Awareness of the inability to allow.
Awareness around thinking we know how it should go.
Awareness of fear.

We may never be completely free of these things. For example, fear is a natural emotion but the issue isn't fear, how we choose to respond to fear has the power to determine whether it becomes an issue. If we don't have awareness then we don't realize we are choosing how we respond to it and that would be the issue. Once there is awareness a greater sense of freedom enters alongside naturally.

My suggestion is that it could be beneficial to run your eyes back over the awareness ingredients and jot down some notes about what each point brings up for you.

Another thing to have awareness of, which we haven't addressed fully yet, is that the Universe is responsible for the thoughts we receive. Yet what we do when working with The Law of Attraction is say, "Aha, I have had a thought, now I must tell the Universe what I want!" This attachment and over identification of the idea as a personal one, is really the main reason it can go so wonky. In a receptive mode our crown chakra is open and the thought travels into our head, then into our heart where we feel inspired to do something, it then travels down through our arms and legs to take action and make it happen.

Yet when we say, "Aha I have had a thought and now I must send it out there to the Universe," the Universe seems to employ the angel of irony!

Might it be the wrong way round to say, "Aha I have had a thought, now I must tell the Universe about it!" if the thought already was communicated to us from the Universe?

In order to increase our consciousness and become free of the angel of irony the first step is to recognise that whatever great idea you have had, has actually come from the Universe and it is now you who is being asked to Co Create your Youiniverse. So it may be better to replace the thought "Oh what a great idea, now I must send that out into the Universe" to "Wow! Thank you Universe, that is awesome! Please guide me on how to Co Create this with you." It shows much more recognition, validation, gratitude and trust/knowingness.

If you sent your idea to someone and they sent it back to you saying, "I have had a brilliant idea! You must help me make it!" Would you feel a bit miffed? If you had the power might you feel a bit like sending the angel of irony to pay them a visit! You might even feel vengeful. Luckily the Universe is much more advanced than we are; it doesn't have an ego and has a far better sense of humour! It manages to find a way to put us back into place through irony. The Universe is not bothered about who owns or identifies with the creation, it has chosen the ones right for the job. The issue is that the way it's worked with, shows a lack of faith. All that is needed is an awareness that it has come to you from the Universe for a reason. The Universe has chosen you to work with it on a Co Creative journey to create your Youniverse. A journey where you feel so totally blessed and excited to have this thought, rather than pressurized to make it happen, and then because you have faith the whole process feels lighter. It becomes a process where you know it will happen because you have been sent it and it would be a pointless exercise otherwise, and also one that knows it is not likely to happen in the way or the time you expect it to!

So may I suggest you go over the list below, and give yourself a mark out of ten for how you felt your awareness of each point was before you began the book. This is just a suggestion and a framework you may find useful because we are our own best judges. Look upon yourself with kind eyes, any change is a good change. Even if it looks as if you have gone backwards, at least now you will have made yourself aware of that and once that has happened you can begin to get on track.

Below is the exercise we did before in the chapter about imagination. Whether you have managed to bring this into your daily routine or not, it is below for convenience sake. By working on this for at least 21 days in a row, you may find your Co Creative ability rises to the next level. For now start by jotting down a mark out of ten for each point, that represents where you were before you started the book. Ten being mastered, zero being at the beginning, and anything else that occurs to you whilst reviewing – just jot it down.

## Daily Practices to Increase Your Co Creative Imagination, Intention, Intuition and Integrity

1. Keep in mind the idea that you are a Youinversal satellite, always connected to the Universe and ready to receive from it at any time, as well as being ready to ask about anything at any time. Release the need for the answer – particularly a need for an instant answer. Just keep yourself awake and open rather than attached. This sets the powerful message to the Universe that you are ready to work in aligned Co Creation. You may get answers coming back and if you do that's great, but the practice is in the opening and the asking.

2. Upon waking from any dreams send your thoughts up and ask what is wanting to come through from that – don't expect to get an answer right away, or at all. It's all in the practice. It can be handy for you to keep a dream journal.

3. As you get dressed notice what clothes you feel drawn to wear. Is it a practical reason? One of social conforming? If so is there something you can wear underneath to help you feel connected to your own individuality? What colours are you drawn to today? Again send thoughts up about why that might be, notice how you are feeling.

4. What thoughts are going on for you about the day? Are they fearful or excited? Depressive or light? If they are

negative get to the root of it; there's going to be fear in there somewhere that you are not going to get what you need and if left to your imagination it can run wild on that unconscious trip, which is the opposite of what we wish to achieve. So if you do feel negative, remember you do have your own hotline to the Universe, and remember that all is not as bad as it seems. How many times do we stress ourselves out over a situation that is not as bad in reality as it is in our heads? Or maybe we stress ourselves out about a situation that has happened. Stop! If it has happened, it's happened. Be kind to yourself and choose good thoughts.

5. Take time to breathe deep, relax and open your heart by allowing yourself to feel the love that is always in there somewhere. Even if you find it hard to do in your current state, the hardest step is to begin; once you have begun you will start to feel better. It is important to connect with the Universe in a relaxed, loving state. I am not one who believes that we have to sit down and dedicate ourselves to a meditation practice in order to do this, if you want to then that's fantastic. I feel the danger is in thinking we have to dedicate time to access that state – so we never really do. I feel it is more important to remember that the most vital thing to do is to wake up to what is running through our head and hearts, and recognize anything that feels heavy. Once we have witnessed that, we can then say, "Ah okay, I am open to this changing." It is that very act of intention that is the catalyst, just like in Quantum Physics as soon as an atom is seen it changes. Meditation increases our awareness and therefore our ability to do this, so if you struggle with natural awareness arising from intention then a meditation practice can help. In fact I do believe meditation has massive benefits for everyone

but not everyone sits and does it, so I am giving you ways to meditate on the move so to speak.

6. Once you have become awake to your thoughts and feelings, you can start to talk to the Universe about what you feel you need, not in a demanding, fearful mistrusting way though. When does talking in that manner to anyone result in success? The Universe is no exception. Practice talking in a way where you clearly and responsibly explain what you feel you need with the energy of confidence and calmness. This is imagination and intention working together at their best. But also remember that you are a micro and the Universe is a macro. Leave room for remembering it knows far more than we do and include that in any communication. State that you are open to receive what you feel you need – or what the Universe knows you need for your highest good and growth.

7. Throughout your day listen to your thoughts and feelings during your activities, if anything feels heavy ask yourself if there is a different way to do this. It's about slowing down enough to have the realizations. Even if you feel you can't change the situation you are in, you can change your attitude to it. Wake up to your feelings, they are an inner compass, if something feels heavy then choose what feels the best for you in that moment.

8. Throughout the day be open and be non-expectant, but ready to take notice of any flashes that happen, albeit visually, auditory or kinaesthetically. And in particular also be aware of your reaction to it. Is there any fear there?

9. Become aware of your self-talk when fear happens, what is it serving? Do you resist it or play yourself down? Criticize it or yourself? Is Judgment arising in you? Do you attach? If so practice changing it to noticing, letting it ride through and saying thank you. It's okay if something you receive isn't in line with what you want, we were given the gift of free will. Just make sure you are releasing it because you really don't want to do it, rather than fear masquerading as you really don't want to do it! Remember you can communicate with the Universe at all times, you can send a message in your thoughts asking why you have been shown this, and what you need to know about it.

10. Most of all, open your heart, open your mind, see each day as a sacred creation and remember your part in it.

## Who is the Cook?

First things first, do you really know who you are? Or are clouded by conditioning and shoulds or shouldn'ts?

These exercises will help you ascertain your real feelings and decipher what is important to you in different areas of your life. It is best done with a partner, but if you can't do so then just be honest with yourself.

1. Firstly from the list opposite, pick out ten values that are most important to you. Number them 1–10, 1 being least important, 10 being most important. Don't get too analytical or change things, just trust what comes up easily and instinctively. Enter these numbers in the column marked 'first response'.

| PERSONAL VALUES | FIRST RESPONSE | FINAL RESPONSE |
|---|---|---|
| Appreciation | | |
| Acceptance | | |
| Belief | | |
| Clarity | | |
| Connection | | |
| Creation | | |
| Compassion | | |
| Co-operation | | |
| Enjoyment | | |
| Empowerment | | |
| Fulfilment | | |
| Forgiveness | | |
| Gratitude | | |
| Growth | | |
| Honesty | | |
| Insight | | |
| Integrity | | |
| Independence | | |
| Justice | | |
| Joy | | |
| Love | | |
| Money | | |
| Patience | | |
| Positivity | | |
| Potential | | |
| Success | | |
| Support | | |
| Trust | | |
| Truth | | |
| Wisdom | | |

2. If with a partner then hand them the book (or sheet if you copied it).

3. Then it is your turn to question you (if you are on your are on your own), or your partner to question you. The process is to compare your first answer against every subsequent answer you have. The question is, "What's more important?" and so on until you have compared all the answers against each other putting a tick the 'final answer' column next to whatever the answer was.

4. Carry on with this process until the first value has been compared to every chosen one.

5. Once you have finished comparing the first value cross it off the list.

6. Move on to the second value and follow the above steps until you have compared every value against every value.

7. Then add up the number of ticks.

8. The one with the most ticks is the most important value; the one with the fewest is the least.

9. How closely aligned with your first answers are you final answers? The more aligned they are the more you know yourself, but don't worry if there was a big difference. By doing this exercise you have already done a lot of re-aligning.

Opposite you will find a career chart and a relationship chart.

| CAREER VALUES | FIRST RESPONSE | FINAL RESPONSE |
|---|---|---|
| Acknowledgement | | |
| Achievement | | |
| Self-belief | | |
| Communication | | |
| Creativity | | |
| Clarity | | |
| Confidence | | |
| Courage | | |
| Enjoyment | | |
| Empowerment | | |
| Encouragement | | |
| Fulfilment | | |
| Faith | | |
| Guidance | | |
| Honesty | | |
| Insight | | |
| Integrity | | |
| Independence | | |
| Justice | | |
| Knowledge | | |
| Money | | |
| Management | | |
| Movement | | |
| Patience | | |
| Positivity | | |
| Praise | | |
| Potential | | |
| Recognition | | |
| Reward | | |
| Success | | |

| RELATIONSHIP VALUES | FIRST RESPONSE | FINAL RESPONSE |
|---|---|---|
| Attraction | | |
| Appreciation | | |
| Beliefs | | |
| Communication | | |
| Connection | | |
| Creation | | |
| Compassion | | |
| Co-operation | | |
| Enjoyment | | |
| Empowerment | | |
| Encouragement | | |
| Flirtation | | |
| Fun | | |
| Growth | | |
| Honesty | | |
| Intimacy | | |
| Integrity | | |
| Independence | | |
| Interests | | |
| Joy | | |
| Love | | |
| Money | | |
| Monogamy | | |
| Patience | | |
| Positivity | | |
| Potential | | |
| Sex | | |
| Support | | |
| Social | | |
| Trust | | |

The above charts are given with consent from a dear teacher of mine Judith Kingdon, and are powerful examples of topics to get clear on about what you value in different areas of your life. They are just examples, feel free to get creative and tailor make as many as you like. These charts are great for aligning your purpose to the Universe, they are fascinating with their ability to reveal the truth about what you really feel and therefore great for your alignment.

Another way to get really very clear on your truth (values) is to elicit a response from the emotions first and then make a chart from those to see what really is your highest priority.

## Emotional Response Exercise

Ask yourself the following questions, and jot down your answers.

1. What makes you feel excited?
2. What makes you feel happy?
3. What makes you feel sad?
4. What makes you feel let down?
5. What makes you feel confused?
6. What makes you feel special?
7. What makes you feel respected?
8. What makes you feel disrespected?
9. What makes you feel angry?
10. What makes you feel hurt?
11. What makes you feel loved?
12. What makes you feel supported?
13. What makes you feel restricted?
14. What makes you feel insignificant?
15. What makes you feel insecure?
16. What makes you feel embarrassed?
17. What makes you feel peaceful?
18. What makes you feel energised?

Take a look at what you have written as your answers. So for instance if you have written that you feel let down when people don't keep to their word then your value might be reliability, trust or honesty, so just jot down which one feels right to you. Do this for all 18.

Make your own values chart out of the emotional responses, and choose your top ten order putting the number 10 as least important and number 1 as most important in the first response chart.

Compare as before.

This exercise, also from Judith, is very powerful in discovering your truth. Once you are in alignment with your own truth you are automatically connected to the Universe from your highest most authentic place and ready to Co Create your Youniverse.

Secondly write a mission statement deriving from the top answers you got, for example if it was career and your top values were creativity, purpose and growth it might be something like…

> *"I am open to receive the work that connects me to the highest good of all, that serves all that I am, that is full of **creativity, purpose** and **growth** for me personally and professionally, and for all that I connect with."*

If you have more clarity about what that is – include it, state working for a certain company for example, nothing wrong with that, as long as you add that you only wish this to happen if it is aligned to the highest good of all.

Allow yourself to play with this mission statement until you feel you have really connected with it from your heart, give yourself permission to get REALLY excited about it, keep re-writing it until you feel that twang.

Let's look at how to twang!

## Co Create Your Twang!

Okay so now's your time to get juicy and feel the emotions you have around your desire…

Close your eyes right now – well actually you need to read this first! So once you have read this, close your eyes and take a few nice deep breaths. Intend that the top of your head is opening to receive your desire, breathe deep down into the heart of you, and as you breathe out feel every one of millions upon trillions of your cells totally buzzing, completely infused with the inspiration of this Co Creation. Next, see and feel the energy of this Co Creation emanating out of your cells and radiating out into your aura. Repeat this process with the rhythm of each of your breaths, building up the energy within and all around so that your aura radiates with this incredible energy, connecting and infusing one and all with the same energy of inspiration, igniting their Co Creation.

It is important to pump up your desire, as that increases your Co Creative ability. Nothing is wrong with desire or will. They stoke the passionate fire of inspiration within. Fire helps us to see where we are going; it warms the soul and brings us back to life. With fire we need boundaries. As the will is the fire, we need to be careful that we aren't coming out of alignment when we feel the fire of the will ignite. We need to remain aware and not leave it unattended; the Universe needs a passionate human who has a will and awareness. Keep stoking your fire, keep attending, keep building, so the flames reach the skies and light the way for all concerned. You can do this by making an offering, a statement to the Universe through ritual. And don't worry, I don't mean that you have to go round the supermarket in cloak and dagger looking for eyes of toads, and wings of bats – although I am not stopping you if that's what floats your boat! (Better leave the dagger at home though.) A ritual is all about intention. You can make anything a ritual, even cleaning the toilet – as long as it's done with intention (which is a great one for getting rid of the crap!). Just take a deep breath in (not specifically talking over the toilet here) and welcome in your connection to the Universe through the top of your head, and then set your intention of what you wish – Co Create your twang! Breathe it out, and then get active! The activity could be a song, a dance, a piece of art, a piece of writing, a piece of craft, or even housework. The process of getting active brings the intention down from your yin (inner) world into manifestation via your yang (external) world.

With this frame of mind we become more aware that everything in life is actually connected to the Universe. Nothing gets in the way; everything is the Universe, everything is a way into our Co-Creation with the right intention. There's no waiting until you've got through the chores, in fact chores become full of meaning that is deep and true cleaning, not just surface. There's no waiting until the kids are in bed, you can Co Create with them. Kids are great at teaching adults about Co Creation, because they are so present in the moment and themselves, their imagination, their play, their own Co Creation. Children have their Universal Satellite switched on. Co Creation is about being connected to the all, the everything, all the time, and consciously recognizing that it doesn't matter what you are doing (within reason) or where you are, just making an intention for connection for the highest good makes it a sacred act.

Almost anything that you decide is appropriate will be, as long as your intention is an offering for the highest good of all, which of course is then born out of humility and respect, not attachment.

Writing is a great way to state something to the Universe. 'Thought, word and deed' is an old magical invocation. So writing has it covered, it's all in the 'spelling!' Give yourself permission to express yourself, no holds barred, knowing that no one has to see it if you don't want to share it.

## Spell Your Future

Start by writing down the very thing you wish to manifest. For example:

"I am open to attracting a decent, loving, committed partner into my life" or "I am open to attracting more love and enjoyment into my life," whichever you feel is most aligned to the highest good of all. If you don't know what you want to attract then just start with something small but random – like a green feather! Have fun with it!

1. Now jot down all the things you're feeling (not thinking) about the area you stated above. Previously, with The Law of Attraction work you may have been taught to concentrate on how you would feel at the time of receiving and we have also done something similar in the Co-Create Your Twang exercise. However, it is also very important that we are not in denial about where we are in the present moment. For connection to happen we need a starting a point, which is reality in the now, the present, and an ending (the dream turning into reality). We then have something to bridge across, to connect. In order to start building we need to do something equally important – face the truth of our emotions in the present. To do this we list how we feel in reality now, the truth of it. Your list may look like this example below:

   Lonely
   Loveless
   Injustice
   Confusion
   Hopelessness
   Despair
   Depression

Anger
Desperation
Fear
Unworthiness
Disbelief
Frustration

Your list may be a stark picture (it may not too), just be real.

2. Now look at that list and see how much passion and inspiration for change is disguised in those feelings, can you see it?
   Lonely = connected, loveless = loved, injustice = recognized, and so on…It's powerful isn't it? This is the Universe giving you all the right ingredients; it's just that we sometimes go the wrong way round with the recipe when projecting how we would feel if we got something. It can be like trying to make a sweet from a savoury, it doesn't work. We have to accept that we have a savoury and devour that before we move on to the sweet. Where projecting can work is when we manage to tune into how we would feel when we attain our dream, and bring that feeling into ourselves in the present moment. But if we are feeling particularly low it can also back fire when we come down, making us feel like our dream is even further out of reach because in reality we feel so far away from that. Our emotional barometer comes back to Earth with a loud bump and a bursting of the balloon. This is why it is important to be aware of the ground and where you are on it.

3. Get clear about what you want. Really clear. And it's better not to phrase it as "I want" because there is a theory that the word want puts it in the future and leaves you

wanting. I am not totally convinced but if there is another word that's better than why not use it? So state "I open my energy to receive…"
Using the partner analogy 'a good partner' just won't cut the mustard. Connect with your heart, feel it, REALLY FEEL IT and allow the information to spill forth. Here is an example…

*"I am open to receiving a life partner who walks beside me, sometimes closely, sometimes in supportive distance.*

*Who sees me, really, really … sees me.*

*Who intuitively feels me, gets me, honours and respects me, loves me wholeheartedly for who I am. All of who I am.*

*Who even loves the parts I struggle with and in turn opens me up to a deeper love of myself, of them and the whole of humanity.*

*Whose love heals my wounds.*

*Who honours my connections with others, teaching me humility and inner security through his own.*

*Who makes me laugh until my sides split, the cows come home, and then some.*

*Who understands and sees the Universe the way I do, but with enough of a difference between us that we help each other's insight increase.*

*Who I trust, totally, completely, implicitly and wholeheartedly.*

*Who is my best friend and there for me through it all.*

*Who I can be truthful with at all times, and know that he will get past any emotional reactions of fear and honour what is coming through for the highest good of all.*

*Who I am in love with as well as like and love with all of my heart.*

*Who makes me feel desired, wanted, loved, respected and special.*

*Who ignites the fire inside of me when he looks at me, and smiles.*

*Who I look at in our daily life and I can feel my heart melt and my attraction ignite.*

*At night, when lying together I can see and feel deeply into his soul and our connection.*

*Whom I can lay naked with and feel totally comfortable with, with no need to add or change anything.*

*A partner with whom I get deeper and deeper connected to as time goes on and with whom I feel more and more ecstasy every time we make love.*

*Who honours and values my freedom and independence as well as our relationship.*

*Who is strong enough in himself, emotionally and financially to withstand the world by himself, yet takes joy in building our path together.*

4. What's your first thought to that? If it is "impossible" then ask yourself why? How sure can you be that it is impossible? That was I writing about my husband. I'm living, breathing proof that it is possible. And if your next thought is "Well maybe it's possible for you but not for me," ask yourself why? Is that really true? How could you possibly know? I once felt that too. Interestingly as mentioned previously, my husband came into my life when I decided for the first time in my life I did not want a partner. But what I really had done for the first time in my life was truly let go. How can the Universe get the message if we are still hanging on one end of the letter?

5. Now it's time for a little meditation...
   After reading this through, close your eyes and take a few deep breaths, give yourself permission to relax and feel the tension release from your head and jaw, down your body and out through your feet.
   Build up that energy of excitement around your creation

and when you can't contain it anymore send it out to the Universe as a rocket full of excitement…
As you truly let go feel yourself becoming totally open and clear.
Now let your imagination run riot with all the things that excite you about it.
Strengthen those scenes and feelings as though you are a magnet for them. Concentrate on the feeling of excitement building within and then letting it go like a supernova, expanding up to the Universe and then sprinkling down all around your world, activating your Youniversal flow.

6. Once you have felt that twang with what you wrote, that's it, that's you shooting that arrow out into the Universe. The next stage is to release it – yes, let go!
I'm aware that telling you to let go can make you wonder if you have managed to or not! So let's concentrate on what you can do afterwards to help that process. Basically the way to let go is to put more direction on where to focus your energy next, rather than spend it wondering if you have let go or not (which can also happen with pelvic floor exercises!). Sometimes within days you can start to see powerful synchronicities around you that are relevant to what you just started to Co Create. Instead of worrying that you may be seeing it in everything and therefore you haven't let go, just change the vibration. See it as a letter back from the Universe letting you know your letter of interest in working in Co Creation with the Universe has been received. A letter that states that the Universe is happy for your participation in the Co Creation of the joint desire of the highest good, and all is under construction. Sometimes there is no synchronistic confirmation, if this is the case it may be

that your Co Creation is not quite in alignment with divine timing yet, or maybe you are not quite in alignment yet, so let's look at some ways you can check yourself and your Co Creation.
Some things to look out for when letting go are:

**Guilt** – who are you to ask for this? What if you getting it takes away from another who needs it? Blah, blah, blah! Guilt is actually one of the most arrogant emotions out there, feeling it implies we know better than the Universe. It is a source of self-esteem damage and when our self-esteem suffers we bring suffering into the world. Guilt is a spiritual arrogance that shows lack of trust in the 'all' and is complete self-abuse, tearing and eating away at Co Creation (yourself and the Universe). The simple fact of the matter is, if you have aligned your Co Creation for the highest good and made sure you have let go of any attachment, then launched it into the Universe with trust that if it manifests it's because it is meant to. And if it doesn't, it's because it's not meant to (at least right now) then that means it will only manifest if it is right, so what is there to be guilty about?

**Prediction** – prediction can make it difficult to let go, it can pull you out of alignment through attachment, so in short prediction can block. Do yourself a favour if you get a prediction and let that go too. Remember quantum physics? As soon as an atom is observed, it changes. This makes prediction very tricky business.

**Rushing!** Yes feeling stressed, like we don't have enough time to be in the present. Allowing our heads to play out that drama stops us from allowing. It was that drama that stopped me listening to the lottery numbers!

## Chapter 9

# The Empress

### Developing a Youniversal Recipe for a Successful Career

> *The law of harvest is to reap more than you sow. Sow an act, and you reap a habit. Sow a habit and you reap a character. Sow a character and you reap a destiny.*
> – James Allen

Welcome to the first chapter where we really look at how to work with Co Creation. So far in the book we have learnt about the necessary ingredients and now we are really starting to put them together. We have already done some Co Creation in our exercises, but the following chapters will demonstrate ways to work with Co Creation that work, and ways that don't!

We are beginning with The Empress, Mother Earth who holds bounty for all. Mother Earth meets our basic fundamental needs so that we may grow in self-sufficiency. We must get our basic needs met first if we are to grow in alignment, and it is all about alignment. We cannot be great Co Creators with a bent aerial! In today's day and age most of us see our 'job' as the thing that meets our basic needs, but sadly not a lot of people feel in alignment with their work.

The word 'job' has a different connotation to 'career'. A job implies it's something you do to earn money and a career implies a sense of devotion, but are there many of us who can even say we are in the right career?

If you feel you aren't in the right job/career then this chapter may bring some stuff up for you, but if you have done the value exercises in the previous chapter then you will be able to see what you value, what makes you happy and aligned, so signposts about the possible directions you could go in for a brighter future may be appearing on the horizon. If you haven't done it yet, I highly encourage you go back and do it before reading on.

We will start with the basic recipe for a successful and aligned career…

### Youniversal Recipe for a Successful Career

*First Ingredient* – A great big dollop of awareness that the right career loves you for who you are, and you love it for what it is. In fact the love is so strong the word career translates into heartfelt service.

*Second Ingredient* – Although the above point is wonderful don't get too comfortable. Add a full dollop of whipped cream on the top, with sprinkles on and see the sacredness in your Co Creation in everything you do. Be present. Be the cream of the crop. Total responsibility rests with you for making the best of your heartfelt service.

*Third Ingredient* – Never over bake your heart into a crust by staying in a situation that makes you unhappy. Always remember that even though it might seem easier to live by using money and being paid (at this current time) your happiness and health is actually priceless.

*Fourth Ingredient* – Honey, the sweetness that makes the world go round is created through the natural joy of buzzing busyness. These days honey is sadly in short supply because our poor bees are suffering at the hands of us humans (a mirror of our own workforce in misaligned conditions). Now, more than ever, we have more reason to nurture the conditions that make honey. Honey is the only food that never goes out of date and bees, well they buzz about with joy everyday – they don't ever have a day off. Ever heard of a bee taking a holiday? No! What a ridiculous idea! Having a day off from your purpose! Yes look after yourself, but if you are in line with your purpose and creation you may feel like a bee. A day off would be absolutely daft, ridiculous and pointless because it would be like misaligning from your purpose for living. The more days off you need the more your vibration is telling you something, like the famous anonymous saying, "Find a job you love doing and you will never need to work again."

Lets quote Bob Marley here too: "The people who want to make the world worse, don't take a day off, so why should I?"

*Fifth Ingredient* – Watch those seasonings of judgment or soon too many will have been added. Piled up high in your recipe it will be too late to get it out! Love your unique Co Creation. That nagging little voice in your head that clings on to all the nit-picky things – that's self-destruction right there. Believe you can have what you want but be realistic in your steps towards it. Put the love of Co Creation in and start walking and working towards your dream. Keep coming gently out of your comfort zone, stretching the boundaries that keep you confined slowly, but surely.

*Sixth Ingredient* – A healthy curiosity about what you are capable of and a mind that isn't listened to when it gives you the messages of "I don't have the money, I don't have the time, I can't do that" blah blah blah! Be curious, how do you know you can't? Even if you tried before and failed that doesn't mean you will now, particularly if you looked at why and learnt from it. Don't be your own prisoner.

*Seventh Ingredient* – Keep your mind on what you can give rather than what you can get, service rather than reward. Have your goals but don't get attached to them. Send out your wishes but let them go. Open up to receiving it (if it is right for you) or something better if the mind is keeping you limited, which let's face it – it probably is. Opening up to receiving means opening up to serving too. The minute we meet someone with the thought "Wonder what you can do for me?" in our heads we are out of alignment. The minute we turn someone away because we can't see how he or she can serve us, we are out of alignment. The minute we are full of joy, wonder and curiosity in any meeting even if we don't quite know the purpose, we are in alignment.

*Eighth Ingredient* – If you don't know what you want to do, don't worry about it or force trying to know what you want to do. Mostly I have seen that people don't know what they want to do when they don't know themselves well enough or because they have gone through so much change. Play, explore yourself, enjoy yourself, join some different groups to see what you like. Travel, make new friends, choose new thoughts, do things differently, give yourself a break, permission to break out of your imposed or old skin. Give yourself a life exfoliation! It's so refreshing!

*Ninth Ingredient* – Allow the freedom to put your own stamp on your recipe and know that your recipe will evolve over time. Don't compare your recipe to others, no competition. If other cooks come to you in the natural flow look at how much more you can create together. Otherwise just keep on aligning to the source and your own creation, minding your own business. You are unique, your purpose is unique and therefore it's the only way to honour you and the Universe.

*Tenth Ingredient* – Cook with love. Love with an open heart, not one that expects, not one that attaches, not one in lack or fear, but one that knows that it beats for itself first and that is why it can open safely. Concentrate on humility, concentrate on service. Not in a way that you are a slave, but in a way that does yourself, the other and the Universe justice. If you ever do not know what to do ask yourself these three questions:

1. What empowers me in this situation?

2. What empowers them in this situation?

3. What is for the highest good of all?

I've yet to see anything but the same answer for all three.

## How to Co Create Success:

**Example 1**

When I first began reading at Mysteries in London I also moved 350 miles away from work – to the very end of Cornwall. The days of the week that I worked in London happened to be the quietest for business and unfortunately the most expensive travel days. I asked Mysteries for a busier day but the answer was that no readers ever gave up those days because it was so busy. So I struggled on for months – really struggled, until I got to the point of utter desperation and asked the Universe instead. I just sent my thoughts up and said, "Look, if it's for the highest good of all I could really do with that Friday!"

The very next day I got a call to say a reader was giving up the Fridays because they had got better-paid work elsewhere for that day, and did I want it!

What did I do right here?

1. I stated what I wanted to the Universe, not to the person.

2. I stated that I trusted the Universe knew better than I what was for the highest good.

3. I didn't concern myself with the how.

4. I opened myself and let go.

**Example 2**

I was desperate to start teaching the psychic arts again as I had done when I had my own centre, I missed it so much. That platform went along with my long-term relationship and I was already teaching healing at Mysteries therefore I couldn't hog all the other courses to myself, it was not my centre. Whenever I tried to teach in Cornwall it didn't work, not enough people, money or strangers! (People knowing each other can be tricky for these types of workshops!)

Once again I was feeling desperation and frustration at an incredibly intense level. I was putting it out to the Universe letting them know what I wanted, but this time I wasn't trusting, I was over concerned with the how as I couldn't see a way.

A few weeks went by and a friend of mine contacted me to say she had landed a job teaching psychic arts but she was leaving the country and thought I should go for it. This friend had no idea how I was feeling. She went on to say the owner had someone for London but maybe she would support me for Cornwall. Well the lady in mind for London ended up dropping out which enabled me to run successful courses at Mysteries in London and in Cornwall!

So what did I do right here?

1. I knew what I wanted.

2. I communicated that to spirit.

3. The power of emotion from desperation and frustration were a powerful activation of my desire. As long as you are being clear about what you feel you need to get out of it, it's like sending a rocket out there. Incredibly powerful.

What did I do wrong?

1. I didn't consciously align or state it to the highest good, but I don't believe that got in the way because it was already aligned to the highest good and my intentions were naturally in alignment on this occasion. Perhaps I was just picking up on what the Universe had in store for me, and the thought and feelings were being channelled down.

2. I also worried about the how. This is something we are told not to do because it is not our job to know how, that's the Universe's job, which is why we need to master the art of letting go.
   I believe I was really meant to teach, hence the huge desire I was feeling and so my asking opened it up for me. It did not matter that I didn't do it correctly, because it was correct. However if you are asking for something that is not completely aligned to your natural state of being in the present, then the conscious work for making it aligned to the highest good is most important and any worry of how it could possibly happen may block. Feelings of frustration, desperation and desire work regardless in my experience, but if you are not using it consciously for the highest good, it can backfire.

## How Not to Co Create Success!

**Example 1**
When I was moving from London to Cornwall I was getting my first website done. I was naïve. I thought all I needed to do was buy a website and I would have an instant online business! There were many delays and as the move got closer I felt more and more fear and frustration, until I got really angry with the Universe and ended up really letting rip! I got my website, but it ended up being £700 for a pretty looking website that was like a car with no wheels.

What Did I Do Wrong Here?

1. I operated from fear.

2. In my frustration and desperation I spoke to the Universe as though I knew what was best for me and it should get out of my way!

**Example 2**
One day I read for a professional gambler and needed to get the bus home after. Well, I missed it and, as it was Cornwall, not London there was a bit of a wait! So I walked into a shop and the lottery desk was literally right in front of the door, so much so that it was hard to enter. There was no time to think about numbers – I was right in front of the desk and the numbers just came in (11, 12, 22, 23, 33, 34).

Well I had a very hard time believing this and said to my guides that they couldn't be right, because they were symmetrical! To which they replied they were the lottery numbers and as they are random they could be symmetrical! So I said I would compromise with them! To which they replied that they were the lottery numbers and you don't compromise with them! But still I put three numbers on one line and three numbers on another line and I made some excuse about being in too much of a rush to change it and went up to the till and put it through – even though every cell of my being was screaming 'NOOOOOOOOOOOO!'

I ended up winning two tenners instead of 4.5 million!

No, I have never had the numbers come to me since, I just stand there marking numbers and knowing they are not right. I go through slip after slip until the cashier thinks there is something really wrong with me and then I give up! However from that experience I do know when I am holding a winning ticket...

Not long afterwards my husband and I got entered for an automatic draw, when they handed me the ticket I said to him, "This is the winning one, I know, I can feel it!" Sure enough it was, but the money we won we lost due to getting conned a few days later!

Not long after that incident I was again rushing (bad thing rushing!) and clicked a link I knew I shouldn't have, yes, instantly hacked. Sitting in the station feeling annoyed at myself again a lady came up to me and handed me a newspaper saying "Loss of 4.5 Million" on the headline!

It seemed the Universe wanted to show me what mind-sets were self-destructive.

They were:

1. Disbelief.

2. Poverty consciousness.

3. "Rational" logic.

4. Rushing.

5. Lack of awareness – not seeing the synchronicity around guiding and linking events.

Below is an exercise that may help you to discover your own self-talk, these exercises are as ever just a possible tool that you might find useful. The scoring is just a framework that could give you a possible workable structure for some definition about who you are and where you are at right now, so you can see how to launch.

## Discover Your Own Success Self Talk

Give yourself –
0 points for strongly disagree
1 point for disagree
2 points for neither agree nor disagree
3 points for agree
4 points for strongly agree

1. I know who I am.

2. I know what I want.

3. I feel the desire burn in me.

4. I get excited thinking about it.

5. I feel inspired thinking about it.

6. I can tell the universe clearly what I want.

7. I can then let it go.

8. I know I don't need to know how.

9. I know I don't need to push.

10. I can relax and trust the process.

11. I know I just need to remain open and aware of what flows into my life.

12. I can relax and allow my energy to receive.

13. I know I must let go of all expectation.

14. I can relax and let go of my own judgments on how things should be.

15. I know I must only concentrate on what my purpose is.

16. I can concentrate on my quality of service and not get pulled off track by others.

17. I can and do feel excited and grateful for every acknowledgment or lesson.

18. I know I must let go of all thoughts of reward.

19. I know I must come from the heart, make decisions with my intuition and I know I do this.

20. I can relax and trust that all will be looked after as long as I do all of the above.

0–20 Points

Allow yourself to make time for you, to find out who you are but not under duress. Allow yourself to have fun, enjoy the pleasure of exploration. Play, create and find out what makes you tick, through fun and only fun! Fun is the beginning of all creation, experimentation is the beginning of all experience, take any pressure off yourself and allow yourself to explore.

20–40 Points
You are getting there but more exploration might just help so read the score above too, start to push your boundaries a little, just gently putting one foot in front of the other, one a day, a small step forward every day. I suggest choosing one of the steps from the list and committing to practicing it for 21 days. Don't be wildly ambitious with this; choose the one that you feel you can achieve comfortably with only a little effort. Use it as a positive affirmation. Write it out on post it note and stick it in places you can see. Once that is mastered move on to the next step.

40–60 Points
Excellent! You are well on your way! If you don't already, then why not start keeping a Co-Creative Diary? Noting down the following points:

- The date of when you get new desires.
- When you speak to the Universe about it, what you asked, and any instant messages/visions/feelings of guidance.
- Any synchronicity regarding it.
- Practice allowing yourself to feel grateful, anytime you worry replace it with gratitude that the thing you are worrying about hasn't happened yet. Practice noticing your judgments, the ones that keep you closed and slowly but surely start changing to open; things should start to come in thick and fast!

60–80 Points
Excellent! What more can I say? You seem to have walked this path for some time already I assume, to develop this amount of trust in the Universe normally takes a lot of lessons and time.

Congratulate yourself and keep up the good work by reading the points in the score above, and strengthening them.

**Tip** – You can also use this list again for other topics, such as relationships, which we will look at next.

# Chapter 10

# The Lovers

## Developing a Youniversal Recipe for Successful Relationships

*Love all, trust a few, do wrong to none.*
– William Shakespeare, *All's Well That Ends Well*

Welcome to the penultimate chapter! Now we have looked at how to Co Create in alignment for the highest good of yourself and others when it comes to career, we will now look at love. Starting with a recipe for graceful relationships…

## A Youniversal Recipe for Graceful Relationships

*First Ingredient* – A great big dollop of awareness that the right person loves you for who you are, no matter what size you are, what quirks you have (in fact they love the quirks) and that they will support you with whatever you go through in your life.

*Second Ingredient* – Although the above point is wonderful, it means you will need a sprinkling of awareness to take full responsibility for making the best of yourself and your life – for the true heartfelt service to yourself and your relationship to ignite.

*Third Ingredient* – Never over bake your heart into a crust by staying in a situation that makes you unhappy, look for a way to change you, where is life asking you to grow towards? All you can do in these situations is to look for the space and glide into it. Remember even though you might be part of a couple, your happiness comes first, and you are the only one who can really truly know what you need to make it happen.

*Fourth Ingredient* – Honey may sadly become in short supply, but that isn't the only sweetness in the world. The honeymoon period may not last, but true love can and will deepen over time; if it is nurtured throughout and not put off until tomorrow when you may have more time, there is only ever today. Funnily enough though, honey is the only thing that never goes out of date. So perhaps it's just a bitter taste that states the honeymoon never lasts; so be open to that too.

*Fifth Ingredient* – Watch those seasonings of judgment or soon you will have too many piling up in your recipe and it will be too late to get it out. Love your unique Co Creation. That nagging little voice in your head that clings on to all the nit-picky things? That's your own self-destruction right there. Relationships are about moving out of the head and into the heart.

*Sixth Ingredient* – A healthy curiosity needs to stay that way and not be overcooked. Want to know if you are with a soul mate? Did you discover that you actually met somewhere before or had the same friendship circles yet never actually met? Lived in the same area or had parallel existences as if you followed each other without knowing it? Do you have any synchronistic history? These are likely markers. But don't get hung up on it...

*Seventh Ingredient* – Don't get sugar confused with salt. Soul mates aren't necessarily life partners. A soul mate is someone who helps your soul evolve through learning lessons, sometimes painful, sometimes joyous, usually both because there is a lot going on between you. Often this means there's a lot to clear before you could ever be together in a completely joyful union (lifetimes of the stuff) and often there is resistance to working through the lessons because of a subconscious fear that once done there will be nothing between you anymore. Take a deep breath and honour the evolution – eventually you will be glad you did.

*Eighth Ingredient* – If you don't follow the recipe to the letter don't worry about it! Just work on releasing your agenda; yes it's good to have a desire, desire ignites attraction and makes things happen – in all areas of our lives. But every time the Universe knows better. Let go of attachments and practice allowing the relationship to show you what it is meant to be rather than the other way around.

*Ninth Ingredient* – Allow yourself the freedom to put your own stamp on your recipe. Always speak your truth, but with respect and compassion. Honesty is the only way you will know that this relationship is right for you.

*Tenth Ingredient* – Cook with love, kneed with love, rise with love... Love with an open heart, not one that expects, not one that attaches, not one in lack or fear, but one that knows that it beats for itself first, and that is why it can open safely. Don't allow fear or attachment to close you down, rejection attracts rejection, be a wayshower and be the change you wish to see.

Did you notice how this is the same recipe? Same ingredients? Just cooked in a slightly different way? What does this tell you? That this maybe the secret recipe to health, happiness, love, success, everything?

## An Example of What to Watch out for when Co Creating in Love

When I was nineteen I went to my first psychic fair, I had a crush on my penfriend in Glasgow at the time (which was the other end of the country to me) and ended up buying a love spell to enchant him. I didn't know what I was doing. It was all made up in a pouch with instructions and I just did it before going out down the pub. That night I met my first husband – who happened to be from Glasgow! After I got married my penfriend started writing me letters about how he wished he had made a move when I visited him and our letters became emotional outpourings – at this time he himself became engaged. My husband found the letters and well that was the end of our marriage. I then asked my penfriend to come and visit but he wouldn't, I became angry with him and that was the end of our five-year friendship. It is important to state that there were also other reasons why my marriage finished, but the point I am trying to make here is:

1. When asking for what you wish for, ask yourself is it affecting another's will?

2. Are you trying to control the outcome?

3. Are you hell bent (pay attention to the words in that phrase) on an attachment to a particular outcome?

4. Is the fulfilment of your need attached to a particular person?

If anything you do is to affect another's will you are effectively practicing black magic and creating a very heavy karmic cross to bear, so it is very important to make sure you have released the need for it to be for a certain person.

You could state: "If it is for the highest good for such and such to be in a relationship with me then I am open to receiving it, *or whoever is right for me right now."*

In the first part of the statement you are aligning to the highest good, letting the Universe know that you understand it knows better than you, and in the last part of the statement you are opening yourself to whatever is right for you right now. This protects you from any karmic backlash.

## How to Heal from Attachments in Love

Fast forward ten years and I had just broken up with my live in long-term business partner and boyfriend. We were together almost seven years and had been best friends for a couple of years before that. We broke up because I had met someone six months earlier – but not in your usual way. The person I met I remembered from a life we shared 400 years previous. One where I was in love with him and these feelings had got intensely confused by the present day meeting. In the present day meeting no words were exchanged because our meeting was a silent movement meditation class. For months I was racked with past life memories and also such a deep connection to him in this life that I knew things about him I couldn't possibly know, especially as we had never exchanged a word! Over the summer, the class had a break and during this time I developed another knowing. A knowing how he was spending his day, every day! It wasn't something I tried to do, it was just happening to me. I had never experienced anything like this before and I felt it meant I should be with him. This was a deeply intense period for me and it hurt like crazy. I thought I was going crazy.

That October I closed my business, my relationship and made myself homeless all in week. A few weeks after that period I sought this guy out and told him everything. It soon became clear that I was in love with who he was 400 years ago and he was a different person now. However he didn't treat me like I had a screw loose and because of this, and the connected feeling that he reciprocated, we became strong friends. The reciprocation was not in the same way as I had felt it, probably due to the fact I was feeling the feelings of a time gone by, which clouded the now. He is still one of my very best friends to this day. However, the whole scenario of remembrance was so very painful that I decided that I did not want another relationship. I did not want to get married. I did not want children. I wanted to go off and travel.

Four months after the breakup of my long-term relationship (and the day after I did a psychic cord cutting ceremony with the person from my past life), I met my now husband, who was not only a dad but had full-time custody of his ten-year-old daughter. I felt our chemistry and connection from the beginning but I decided I just wanted to be friends and tried to deny what I was feeling. I felt it wasn't the right time because of all I was going through. But he was such a nice guy that when he asked me out I couldn't bear to say no to him! And I knew from then that was it.

I was still in a lot of heartbreak and so every morning in the shower I prayed. I prayed that I could love all three of them in the way I was meant to (my ex, the guy from the past life and my future husband) and that we would all find peace in the situation. Now all three of them are deep friends of mine to this day (husband included in that account) and both my ex and the man from the past life attended our wedding and get on really well with my husband. In fact the past life connection is my husband's favourite friend of mine. And me? Well I am very much at peace and happy, knowing I am with the right man for me.

So what did I do right here?

1. I stated what I wanted – which was a spiritual wish for unity and peace.

2. I asked for help to love them in the way that I was meant to (releasing attachment/agenda).

3. I didn't concern myself with the how.

4. I opened myself and let go.

Another interesting point here is that I did not want children OR marriage of domesticity but I got it! Perhaps for two reasons:

1. I had truly let go.

2. The Universe gave me what I needed rather than what I thought I wanted.

Interestingly enough, a very similar past life scenario happened to me several years later, one of which I have come through with yet another very deep friendship. And even though I had been through it once before and had learnt a lot about how intense feelings don't necessarily equate to 'they must be my life partner'. Even though I knew from last time that deep intense feelings upon meeting someone is just your soul recognizing them from before. Even though I knew deep down I was already with the man who was absolutely correct for me in this lifetime and I loved with all my heart, I didn't find it any easier, any less painful, or less confusing. Nor did the process speed up because I had been through it once before. What became clear was that I had to go through it. There was no other way, no fast forward button just because I had seen a similar movie before.

I think what I am trying to say is don't expect letting go of any intense emotions to be easy, especially if there is a strong feeling of confusion attached to them and especially at the beginning, because it can feel like such a shock. But let go you must, only by truly letting go can you really see if they are meant to be in your life at all. Take a deep breath and jump … sometimes that jump needs to be broken down into bunny hops, and that is fine, as long as you keep moving a little bit at a time.

The number one area people consult me about is of course hands down, love and relationships. Just like the number one thing to make films or music about is, yes, love and relationships. This is the power of the heart. The heart is our most powerful organ. Not only physically, but emotionally, magically, spiritually, Co Creatively. Love, as they say, makes the world go round. And it makes us go round and round until we get really dizzy, lose all direction and finally collapse in a heap. Nothing can make you lose your head like intense feelings, nothing can close you down like intense feelings, and nothing can open you up like intense feelings either. Perfectly sane people commit completely insane acts in the name of 'love'. But love is not love if we are losing our alignment and feeling the need to possess a person. Possession is a better word to describe such a feeling.

My belief is that when we meet a strong connection we become overloaded by internal processes. Sub conscious atoms say, "I remember you" and the conscious atoms feel a boom of chemicals, the combination is enough to give the most stable person a run for their money. And then we either fall head over heels or completely cut off. It's like we can't stand being in that place of not knowing and letting go of our agendas, standing there naked, open in wonder and excitement about what the relationship will reveal to us just feels way too intimidating. It seems we would rather try our damnedest to mould it into what we want it to be. Whether you freeze, run or control it really doesn't matter, all these scenarios are not subtle enough to see what sacredness lies within the connection. What I find the most heart-breaking thing about today's society is "you must fit my agenda, or I don't want to know you culture". That may sound harsh, but I have lost count of how many times I have been asked if such and such would live up to what they want, and if the cards indicate the possibility of that not happening, then the person decides they no longer want that relationship in their life. Only today I had this very scenario:

A lady came to me to ask about a guy she liked but was upset about because it didn't seem to be reciprocated. When I mirrored back to her that he liked her a lot but it didn't seem to be romantic, her answer was "What's missing?" And I said, "What do you mean?" She looked at me confused, and I looked back at her confused, then said, "Look, here with him you have an apple, not an orange. Nothing's wrong with the apple, nothing's missing from it, it's just not an orange."

Once she got it she decided she would chuck the apple away and get an orange. She couldn't see that she can have an apple AND an orange! Now, this is the person's right or choice of course. But I just find it so very sad that today's perceptions around relationships are so conditioned.

We seem to preach unconditional love, yet go into friendships or relationships with a big list for the person to live up to. And when they don't they suddenly become disposable, their head being decapitated with one foul cross off the death sentence list. If it is that we meet everyone for a reason then how on Earth are we going to find out that reason if we go into relationships like this? How many amazing treasures lay discarded on the dump? The treasure of spiritual and emotional development, and is there any better treasure than that?

Friends and psychics in the past have told me I should just cut people out my life and I have been accused of having a problem with separation when I wouldn't do it. When I challenged them on how I wasn't going to do that, the answer was "Well of course you can keep them in your life but it will be harder." Well yes it may well be harder in the short term, but in the long term I know I will grow from this and I know my life will be richer for the experience and for the on-going connection too. It's tough, keeping your head/awareness in relationships and not feeding your agenda. But it gets easier with time and then the most amazing thing happens. The space between you when no longer filled with agenda becomes full of sacredness, an unspoken deep feeling, a knowing that you are on a journey together, an adventure of discovery about yourselves, each other, the world, and the Universe. The feeling of openhearted surrender to the divine and each other is a much higher feeling than the low addicted pulls of agenda. And if you are really willing to look at what the relationship is showing you, rather than what you want it to be then your own personal transformation from the journey is tremendous! Yes it's hard work, but so totally and utterly worth it.

Of course there is the other side of the coin too, the one which doesn't cut a person out when they don't meet the agenda, but still the attachment to the agenda is the issue. Here is the scenario:

You really like someone, there is a connection there but you have an agenda that they aren't living up to, yet you like them so much you can't bear to let go. So you attach to them and your agenda with even more vigour than ever, thinking you can change them. How do you know when you are doing this? Obsession, control, stress, anxiety and basic unhappiness pulsate through you because you are displaying a basic disregard for everything, yourself, your life, the Universe and the other person.

Maybe if you could see you can't make an apple an orange, you would then stop trying to make an apple an orange (which of course is a complete waste of time) and go to the shops to get an orange. But! Remember you can have an apple AND an orange! Your life might even be all the more juicier for it! No one ever said you must only eat apples or oranges did they? Am I missing something?

Accept the apple, get the orange and enjoy them both for the different flavours they bring to your life. Arguing with reality is very pointless madness, isn't it? If we saw someone saying to an apple, "You are an orange," over and over again, we would think they had gone mad, wouldn't we?

## How to Get over an Apple Not Being an Orange

## Fake It to Make It

Have you ever heard the phrase "fake it to make it"? I know you have. Essentially that's what we do with positive affirmations – we phrase in the here and now that we are feeling a way that we aren't, but over time by stating it we find we actually do start to feel it. It's the same here; you may not feel like opening yourself to anything other than your attached desire. But if you want to align to your truth, purpose, your eventual happiness and what is right, then reality says there is no other way. So start telling yourself you are so over it even if you aren't, just that very message will activate powerful shifts within, and that is the beginning of the faking it becoming the making it. You may feel resistances to that process, but...

## Release Your Attachment

Attachment blocks anything coming to you, even your very desire. Your desire might be meant to be at some point but your desire can and will block it if you are grabbing onto it so much that you can't let go and relax to receive. Real love is like the art of real listening, open your ears, clear out your judgments, open your mind, open your heart, receive whatever is being said or shown, see the gift in the present moment. Listening is hard. Real listening that is. We automatically stop listening before someone has stopped talking because we are busy formulating our judgments and reactions to articulate our answer. Our heads become packed with thoughts, our opinions, our agendas, our projections and our conditions.

Yet to me it seems there is no greater thing to work on than the art of listening. When we consciously work on listening all time stays still, you become present and deeply connected with that person, sacredness hangs in the air and a compassion and empathy spill forth from your heart. I'm not there yet (I am a Leo with Mercury in Virgo and Mars in Gemini!), but I am committed to doing this. For me learning to really listen is learning to really love. And I am not just talking about listening to another human, I am also talking about learning to listen to the guidance within and all around you. Learning to listen to the Universe, which is what this book is all about, listening and loving you, life, people, the Universe and all that you are in a Co Creative partnership with.

## A Little Exercise for Releasing

1. When you wake up, take note of your first thoughts and feelings, do they feel light or heavy? If you feel heavy know this is karma, it's something to clear.

2. Anything that feels heavy needs clearing, as soon as you have a little time by yourself – even if it's just in the shower – surrender your will up to the divine and pray that you are helped to feel the goodness, peace and release. Know that you are guided through this situation in the way that is for the highest good of all concerned, and that your desires are released from you.

3. Be patient and loving with yourself, telling yourself you should know better or you should be over it by now isn't going to help. You are going through what you are going through for a reason, and it will take however long it takes. As long as you keep up the second step you are working in alignment, and you will be clearing as effectively as you can – for the highest good of all involved.

## Finally...

Work on being whole in yourself, let go of needing love from the outside, and you will attract that which you have become, an amazing partner with so much love to give, because you have love for yourself overflowing from you naturally. It's a natural law I feel, and it is the best present you can give to yourself.

Give yourself the gift of love today, make today the first day of the rest of your life, and turn it within, strengthen your own heart with love, so that the Universe says "Wow! The quality of love brimming from that person means we have to send them someone who deserves such a high quality."

These aren't just words, I've lived it.

# Chapter 11

# The Star

## Finally, a Channelled Recipe for Igniting Your Youniverse

*Your life has an inner purpose and an outer purpose. Inner purpose concerns being and is primary. Outer purpose concerns doing and it is secondary. Your inner purpose is to awaken. It is as simple as that. You share that purpose with every other person on the planet – because it is the purpose of humanity. Your inner purpose is an essential part of the purpose of the whole, the universe and its emerging intelligence. Your outer purpose can change over time. It varies greatly from person to person. Finding and living in alignment with the inner purpose is the foundation for fulfilling your outer purpose. It is the basis for true success. Without that alignment, you can still achieve certain things through effort, struggle, determination, and sheer hard work or cunning. But there is no joy in such endeavor, and it invariably ends in some form of suffering.*

– Eckhart Tolle

After writing about the mis/re/alignments of 11 and 111 as a symbol of what has happened in the world and coming back into alignment of the 1 in service with Co Creation (11), it seems only natural and right that this book should conclude on chapter 11. You are 1 and the universe is 1, Co Creation is 11. So below, is a little communication between myself and the Universe on staying aligned, honouring yourself and the Universe, reaching your highest potential and living your Youniversal life, full of magic and purpose.

**8 October 2013**

Dear Universe,

I am not sure I have ever really written to you before to tell you how incredible you are, how much I thank you and how much love and gratitude I feel for you. I guess at age thirty-six it's about time I did! Even though you know I know you think that, and I know you know that!

I know and you know that I am far from perfect!

In my daily rush and pressures I do things to you which don't honour you, like going to the supermarkets, not doing enough recycling and buying things with lots of packaging or products that may not be ethically traded. And that's only the things I am conscious of, the thought of the amount of wrong-doing I do through my unconscious state scares me and not just to the economy, or the outer physical world, but to my relationships and myself. Yet I know you love me unconditionally and hold me for all that I am and I hear you telling me not to be too judgmental or hard on myself, but to think only thoughts that make me feel good.

I want to ask you what you need from us for once, instead of hearing all of us praying for our needs to be met. But before I do, I want to thank you for always answering the prayers that were/are meant to be answered.

As an only child who was different to all the other kids and being raised in a single parent family I often felt very alone, even when the supernatural events happened. I couldn't understand them at the time, just like I didn't understand why everyone around me had 'normal' families and friends.

I showed great disdain for you and life as a child, even to the point of trying to take my own in my youth.

It was only at twenty, when you gave me the soul to look after that we called Lauren that I knew I had to work at understanding you more. That if I didn't then I knew my life would truly be over.

Since that time I have become increasingly aware of your love and support and I feel my understanding of you has grown immensely, although of course it still has eons to go. I know you have gone out of your way to show me you have my back and for that I am immensely grateful.

I may not always like what you do, but I have come to understand that there is a higher reason even if I don't understand it, or I can't see it. I have come to trust you implicitly…

(It is here that I try to continue to write but the feeling of response from the Universe comes in and overpowers it, in other words, I hadn't planned to stop here.)

Dear Tiffany,
We know life on Earth is not easy, your bodies hang round you like big rubber suits anchoring you deep down to the ground. Even without the conscious remembrance of being bodiless they can still feel so heavy and restrictive and increasingly so as you age. This is why it is so very important to treat your bodies well by drinking water, eating good vibrant fresh food – not too little and not too much. Yoga is an incredible exercise for keeping your bodies in alignment to us (that which you call the Universe or Creation). Just ten minutes a day is enough to start right…

And we haven't even started looking at emotions and we won't be talking about emotions here because the darker emotions are your own barometer for showing you that the above is out of balance. You are in a physical body in a physical world. Look after your physical body and you will look after the world.

This is what we want people to know…

That changing the world starts with the most basic care of 1-self. There is so much distraction planted around in your world to keep you off balance yes, but in the bigger picture this is all part of the greater plan. It's all about consciousness raising. We know you have been aware that we have been downloading new energies through to the planet to help this. We know you are aware of the shifts that have been taking place as we see you witnessing people shifting in to far more holistic health and we feel your joy at this. That is enough thanks for us.

Soon people will find it much easier to make beautiful conscious choices in their lives. Choices that are full of love for 1-self and that will reverberate round the planet. Things like unnatural food, products and money are losing their power and will become obsolete.

You have shown much commitment to getting this book written for us and we see how much you've struggled. Feeling like you hadn't done enough, that the book wasn't clear enough, that you needed more knowledge.

Those very thoughts made it so hard to get through to you. You yourself wrote in this book about the state of judgment and how it keeps you blocked. Yet you did it to yourself. This is not said with blame, we are reflecting to you in order to raise consciousness. And of course you will lose it again and of course that will be fine too, for it really is all part of the master plan.

We had much delight this afternoon when whilst brushing your teeth you finally heard that all you were to do was write a letter. You didn't know why you had to do that, yet you knew you just had to do it and we felt your joy when we took over and started writing back to you even before you thought you had finished. And you know that is all you have to do, you just have to allow a feeling and follow it, you don't need to understand it, or even try to, and you definitely don't need to judge it.

Even though you still do judge, you are one of the ones that judge yourself less, you have a strong ability to listen to your feelings and follow them. In fact you know we made you feel like doing anything else is impossible!

You see, that is what we need. It's easier to Co-Create with humans that have those abilities.

Fear is an issue, fear is the root of all problems and it is something we are working on so strongly to clear. Yet the harder we work on it, the more the battle comes on strong. This is nothing new, the dark and the light. It has always been there, always been the same. But it is not always destined to remain the same. This is another judgment (judgment arises from fear) we are working on. The way you humans think that things will always be the way they have always been, keeps you so very closed to hearing us.

It's important that you listen to your body – regularly check in to how it feels and what it is telling you. Your body contains all you need to survive, not just physically, but mentally, emotionally, spiritually, you are your own world. If you learn how to look after your own world then the world your body lives in would be the world we are waiting for. Learn to look after your own world and you will see heaven here on Earth.

You are made out of stardust and the wisdom held within you is infinite. Your body is incredibly wise, do what makes you feel good and do whatever you can to honour that feeling in that moment. Feeling good is not about feeling lazy, spoilt or feeding an addiction. That is trying to cover up a bad feeling. Real feeling good is about feeling growth.

So when you ask what it is we need, that is it. Awareness of the above is all.

You do not need to write more.

With infinite love.
Yours sincerely,
The Universe

## Other Books in This Series

### *The Transformational Truth of Tarot*

*The Transformational Truth of Tarot* teaches Tarot in a way never done before. Rather than list meanings, it shows the reader how to bring the Tarot alive, and how to feel and understand it deeply through their own experiences by using a series of enlightening exercises. The Tarot is a reflective tool, a mirror, we need to look at ourselves in the face of it for true transformation to take place – here is how.

This book does not tell you what the meanings are; it reflects it back and fosters inner revelations, causing the Tarot to become alive, moving with the flow and flux. *The Transformational Truth of Tarot* is a ground-breaking non-fiction book that illustrates the intriguing system of Tarot in a whole new light; not only as a predictive tool but as a philosophy that underpins our entire existence.

*The Transformational Truth of Tarot* was released in 2012 and won an Award for best spiritual book of that year.

ISBN 978 1 78099 636 3

Axis Mundi Books provide the most revealing and coherent explorations and investigations of the world of hidden or forbidden knowledge. Take a fascinating journey into the realm of Esoteric Mysteries, Magic, Mysticism, Angels, Cosmology, Alchemy, Gnosticism, Theosophy, Kabbalah, Secret Societies and Religions, Symbolism, Quantum Theory, Apocalyptic Mythology, Holy Grail and Alternative Views of Mainstream Religion.